# RAPTURED

# RAPTURED

Thomas S. McCall
and
Zola Levitt

**RAPTURED**

© 1975 by Zola Levitt Ministries, Inc.
Dallas, Texas

Library of Congress Catalog Card Number 75-15481
ISBN 0-89081-014-1

**Printed in the United States of America.**

**DEDICATED**

*to all of those who are looking forward to that day when they will be Raptured by the Lord Jesus Christ.*

# CONTENTS

# INTRODUCTION

*Raptured* is the third book on Bible prophecy by the team of Dr. Thomas S. McCall and Zola Levitt. In each of these books we have concentrated on a single issue of Bible prophecy, presenting the subject in full-length form and putting it into easily understood language.

Our hope is to explain things people need to know in words they can understand.

In many ways *Raptured* has been the most enjoyable of the three books we have written, mainly because it covers a much happier subject than the previous two books. *Satan in the Sanctuary* deals with the tragic desecration of the future tribulation temple, and *The Coming Russian Invasion of Israel* was certainly no happy matter to discuss!

But who could have anything against the Rapture? What a happy hope it is, and what a pleasure it is to study it and to write about it! The Rapture will be a work of the Lord, while our other books described works by the Devil. What a difference this makes!

We have introduced scenarios at the beginning of each chapter to dramatize the subject of the chapter. You can get the gist of each chapter in short-story form and share our own excitement about the Word of God. The scenarios were mainly the idea of our editor and publisher, Bob Hawkins—as talented a man as God ever selected to distribute books.

We are often asked how two men write one book. Very simply, Dr. McCall is a theological writer and Mr. Levitt is a popular-style writer. McCall formulates the initial ideas, the Biblical material, the concepts, the arguments, and the conclusions. He then presents this manuscript to Levitt, who reworks the material into a highly readable, clear, and entertaining book. The spiritual and practical partnership of McCall and Levitt may be leading to the realization of a life's ambition for each of them—McCall is becoming a pop writer and Levitt is becoming an informed theologian.

We say all this because we wish that others in the Christian writing fields would try dual authorship. The written word is essential to the propagation of the gospel in today's world; it was initially God's own way, and we feel it is still one of God's best ways. But we feel that Christian book must compete in the open book market with secular books; they must be as well-written, informative, and understandable as any book that can be picked up in a drugstore or super-market. The enemy is a clever writer too, and we must be able to reach his faithful audience. We must communicate as well as he does.

Because not all theologians are writers, and vice versa, we wish that many of our brothers in the faith would team up to reach the highest number of readers. To us, this serves the Lord best.

There are many Christian ministries, the Scriptures tell us, and we feel that research, writing, marketing, selling, advertising, printing, and all the functions of getting the Word to the public in books are holy callings. We feel that each man should faithfully pursue his part in the total effort of moving the huge part of this world that is struggling along with only the vaguest understanding of God and His plans.

# Chapter 1

# GOING UP!

*Gone!!*
*Vanished!!*
*The young executive yawned slightly as he entered the familiar lobby of the office building at the start of another routine day of business. He scarcely acknowledged the presence of the elevator dispatcher, who gestured to an open elevator and said, "Going up." He certainly didn't imagine that the dispatcher's familiar call, "Going up," was prophetic and would be fulfilled at once!*

*Somewhere around the tenth floor he heard an earsplitting shout and the unmistakable sound of a trumpet blast overhead. And then he really began going up!*

*Before he could blink his eyes, or wonder if the others in the elevator had heard the strange sounds, the young executive was shooting up the elevator shaft. He seemed to take off like a rocket, going right through the top of the elevator and continuing right through the top of the building itself! He was careening upward through the bright morning sunshine and enjoying a completely euphoric feeling of well-being.*

*He was dumbfounded, but he was loving it! All around him he saw other people accelerating through the air, and they glowed white. They shined like silver against the blue sky. He suddenly realized that he too was "shining" in this peculiar way, and that his body had somehow been changed.*

*Before his mind could put it all together, his eyes looked upward and saw what was drawing him and all the others into the sky like a gigantic magnet.*

*There He was! Jesus Christ Himself!*

*The Lord Jesus in all His magnificence stood resplendent in the air as the believers rose to meet Him. He was more glorious, more brilliant, more lustrous than the man had ever imagined He would be, yet there He stood in plain view.*

*The sight set the man's mind functioning again and he understood instantly that he was in the Rapture. He realized that he and the other believers around him in the air had suddenly become "like Jesus," seeing Him face-to-face and possessing their new resurrection bodies.*

*It was true! The promise was real and it was being fulfilled!*

*He knew well enough what the so-called Rapture was, ever since he had come to believe in Jesus Christ a few years before. And he had believed in this remarkable event implicitly, as he believed all of what the Scriptures taught. But he had been puzzled,* too. *Was it going to happen in the incredible way that the Bible said it would? Would he really rise into the air and meet Jesus personally on the clouds? Would he be alive then, and conscious of what was happening?*

*Now he had his answers. Today was the day, and he was alive and well. And there was the Lord, just as He said He would be. He promised to return and receive His own, and here He was, keeping that one-of-a-kind promise.*

*The joyful company of believers assembled around the Lord high above the earth. As the Master greeted them they were overwhelmed by the warmth of His enveloping love. Then Jesus turned away from planet earth and led His church away to the place He had prepared for them.*

*Back in the elevator, a few people were rather incredulous. Not everyone had noticed the strange turn of events, since they were mostly looking down at their shoes, like people in elevators do! But some had clearly seen the young man with the attaché case get on at the first floor, and they certainly hadn't seen him get off. And yet, he was gone.*

*Oh well, another day, another dollar. They all got off at their various floors and went about the day's business. Those who thought they were seeing things took a tranquilizer or phoned their analysts. The others had perceived nothing of the godly events, then or ever before, and they weren't bothered at all.*

*They failed to appreciate that the time of God's wrath upon the earth was about to begin.*

*If any of them were to survive the next seven years it would truly be a miracle.*

That fantastic scenario is a Bible-based hope for millions of believers in Jesus Christ around the world. They would not find that description of events strange at all, in view of the Scriptural teachings about the Rapture of the church. In fact, they wait to play their part in it.

These Christians hold that a transforming experience like the one we described above will culminate the church age, and that all believers in Christ will be taken to glory with Him. This will happen before the Lord allows the horrendous events of the Great Tribulation to convulse the earth.

They eagerly await this life-changing development and they refer to it as "The Rapture."

## WHAT'S IN THE WORD?

The Bible indeed teachers this doctrine of the taking out of the church by Christ. We have based our dramatization on the description in the Word.

The term "rapture" does not actually appear in English translations of the Scriptures, but the Apostle Paul used the expression "caught up" in his description of this unique event (1 Thessalonians 4:17). The Latin Vulgate Bible utilized the word *rapere* for "caught up," and the English word "rapture" was taken from that. It's rather a romantic word, considering the event, but it has survived the centuries.

Paul's description is fascinating:

> For the Lord himself shall descend from heaven with a shout, with the voice of the archangel, and with the trump of God; and the dead in Christ shall rise first, then we who are alive and remain shall be caught up together with them in the clouds, to meet the Lord in the air, and so shall we ever be with the Lord. Wherefore comfort one another with these words.
> —Thessalonians 4:16-18

The main thrust of this particular reference to the Rapture concerned the dead believers, or those who had passed away on earth in faith. Were they to lose out on meeting the Lord? The Thessalonian church had addressed this matter to the inspired apostle, who set their minds at rest.

Clearly, ". . . the dead in Christ shall rise first, then we who are alive. . . ." the *souls* of dead believers are already in the presence of the Lord, and will return with Him at the Rapture. These souls will be reunited with their bodies then, which will be resurrected and caused to rise ahead of the living believers at the time when all are "caught up."

We can conclude that the dead believers will be honored rather than losing out, and that we need have no concern over the fate of passed-on believers. Also, whether we are alive at the time of the Rapture or we die before it is immatieral; all believers will participate in the order in which they lived. All believers can look forward to the shout and the trumpet.

During the dramatic events of the final Passover week in our Lord's earthly ministry, His disciples had much cause for concern. The Lord announced His imminent departure clearly and had instructed His followers that this was for the best He comforted them greatly in the upper room discourse with His own intimation of the coming Rapture:

> In my Father's house are many mansions; if it were not so, I would have told you. I go to prepare a place for you. And if I go and prepare a place for you, I will come again and receive you unto myself, that where I am, there ye may be also.
>
> —John 14:2, 3

This was Jesus' farewell address to the faithful, and they took heart from it.

In addition to his remarks to the Thessalonian church concerning the details of the Rapture, Paul also described the event for the Corinthians:

> Behold I show you a mystery: we shall not all sleep, but we shall all be changed, in a moment, in the twinkling of an eye, at the last trump; for the trumpet shall sound, and the dead shall be raised incorruptible, and we shall be changed.
> For this corruptible [flesh] must put on incorruption, and this mortal must put on immortality. So when this corruptible shall have put on incorruption, and this mortal shall have put on immortality, then shall be brought to pass the saying that is written, Death is swallowed up in victory.
>
> O death, where is thy sting? O grave, where is thy victory?
>
> —1 Corinthians 15:51-55

This passage deals especially with the remarkable metamorphosis to be undergone by believers "in the twinkling of an eye" at the Rapture. Whether living or dead ("We shall not all sleep"), we will be changed into immortal beings at that moment. The dead in Christ will have their bodies raised "incorruptible"—impervious to physical deterioration—while the living will "put on immortality" and become immune to death.

Like the Lord, we will all defeat death. This is the ultimate victory over the grave, which has so far dominated men completely. At the Rapture death loses its sting and the grave loses its victory.

## COME FLY WITH US

Are you on the passenger list?

It's obvious from the Scriptures we have quoted that the passenger list for the Rapture is highly restricted. In a word, it's restricted to believers.

We can only regret the exclusion of the unbelievers, since they will be left behind to face the Antichrist and the Tribulation period. (We will discuss various views of the time of the Rapture relative to the Tribulation period in a later chapter).

The passenger list is restricted in other ways. The believers involved in the Rapture will be only those of the church age—from the day of Pentecost, when the Holy Spirit came (Acts 2), to the day of the Rapture. There are other believers to consider—those of the Old Testament times and those who trust Christ during the Tribulation period itself and the Millennium to follow it.

These "early and late" believers will all be accounted for in God's promise, however. Daniel 12:2 indicates that the Old Testament saints will be raised from the dead in connection with the establishment of the Messianic kingdom when Christ returns to the earth. These believers of bygone times will join us in the Millennium, happily. (Daniel has less happy news for old Testament *unbelievers*—"shame and everlasting contempt"!)

Believers of the Tribulation times will appear as the sheep in Jesus' judgment of the sheep and the goats (Matthew 25:31-46), and they will be ushered directly into the kingdom at that time. The goats will not make it. (See chart on page 21.)

For those alive today the very best option is the Rapture. To await the Tribulation period and then contend with the hard times, whether in faith or otherwise, is foolhardy.

Are you on the passenger list? Are you inscribed

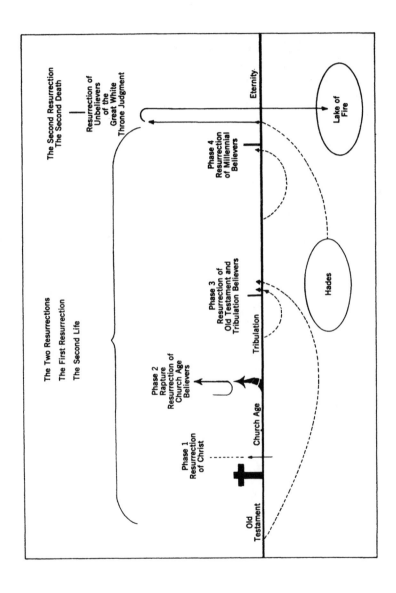

in the Book of Life? Have you received Christ? Believing in Christ in the only charge for your ticket.

Take care of that now.

Come fly with us!

# Chapter 2

# THE FEASTS AND THE FUTURE

*It had been a good year.*

*Baruch sat back against his barn in contentment on this last day of the harvest. He was perspiring heavily, but he felt deeply satisfied. It had been a good crop, and the last sheaf of wheat was now stacked in the barn. There would be plenty of wheat for the offering at the Feast of Tabernacles, plenty for the family's winter needs and plenty for his few cattle and sheep. His little piece of ground near Bethlehem wasn't the most fertile farm in Judea, but it was dependable and he had much to be thankful for.*

*His son Isaac had turned 13 during the summer, and it would be an especially exciting fall festival season this year for that reason. Isaac was now a man and would enter the Court of the Men for the first time this Feast of Trumpets. How that boy* yearned to hear the sound of the trumpet!

Isaac had been with the children during the Passover celebration, the Feast of Unleavened Bread and the Feast of Firstfruits, earlier that spring, and he could talk about nothing else but his coming maturity in the seventh month.

It took Baruch back in time. He too had gone with his father to the feasts three times each year. They would journey to Jerusalem—not a long trip from their rural home—and they would meet brethren from all over Israel and even from foreign countries. Baruch would watch his father get the appropriate artifacts and sacrifices together for each trip, and he would dream of the day when he himself would go up to King Solomon's Temple to worship the Lord of Hosts.

They used to go to Jerusalem, as the Law required, for the three spring feasts, for the Festival of Weeks, (toward the beginning of summer), and for the three fall feasts. These were always joyous occasions, and their sanctity was not lost on young Baruch.

But now he himself was the father, and it was his own son who exulted in the coming pilgrimage to Jerusalem. It was wonderful to be a Jew and to know that God was faithful and that the land would go on for all time.

Soon the trumpet would sound. Baruch would barely hear its piercing tones from the Temple, some five miles distant, but he could picture the old priest standing high on the Temple wall holding the long shofar aloft. Not every Jew lived where he could hear this Temple trumpet, and Baruch was glad to be in Bethlehem. The little city was not really special among the many towns and villages of Israel, but Baruch was happy here, near the Temple of God.

There was a legend about the trumpet of the Temple. It was said that it was Joshua's own trumpet, which he used to blow down the walls of Jericho some six centuries before. Joshua had brought his people into their promised land at the sound of the trumpet!

But all that was ancient history. There were things to be done now in order to be ready to leave immediately when the trumpet sounded. Baruch was glad to have completely finished the harvesting of his fields (Isaac was big enough to be of real help now) because the harvest had to stop at the sound of the trumpet. He knew they would see some workers still in the fields as they went along the road to Jerusalem, but these were not Jews. Some of the foreigners who worked the lands would stay to complete the harvest, and they did not respond to the trumpet call, of course. Occasionally there would be two men working side-by-side in a field—a Jew and a foreigner. The trumpet would sound and the Jew would leave at once, while the stranger stayed in the field. That was Trumpets—a rather "sudden" feast.

And suddenly he heard the trumpet! Just a small sound in the distance, so that at first he thought it was his imagination. But the steady, staccato blasts were unmistakable. This was the time; now was the hour. Isaac and Baruch would now make for Jerusalem with all speed, witnessing together the priest's choir, the Levites at their sacrificial duties, and the collected worshipers of all Israel. Now a man, Isaac would prepare with his father for the awesome Day of Atonement (to come ten days after the Feast of Trumpets), and then they would live *for another week in the booths set up for the observance of the Feast of Tabernacles.*

*The trumpet was sounding! God was calling all Israel to come home—home to Jerusalem, home to the House of the Lord.*

Because the Rapture concerns only the New Testament church, Bible students have generally assumed that information about it is found only in the New Testament.

But, in a wonderful way, God wove the principle of this mighty culmination of the church age throughout the Old Testament as well. An imaginative Bible scholar of the first century, having only the Old Testament to study, might well have arrived at this principle by thinking about trumpets.

(The accompanying chart shows the feasts, their various dates, and the symbols they represent.)

The trumpet which sounds at the moment of the Rapture is the key to understanding a vast panorama of spiritual depth, beauty, and magnitude. The Person and work of Christ in all ages, and

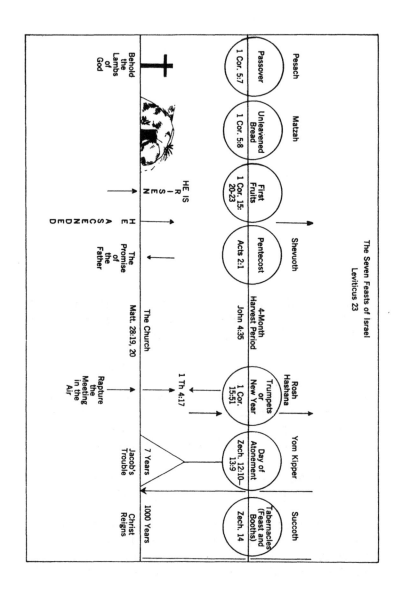

The Seven Feasts of Israel
Leviticus 23

| Pesach | Matzah | Shevuoth | | Rosh Hashana | Yom Kipper | Succoth |

God's very plan for redemption, are fully explained through the complete understanding of this unique symbol.

We have to go all the way back to the Book of Genesis for the first reference to the trumpet and its use in a redemptive way.

Then too, we all know the story of Joshua, the great Jewish general who frustrated the defense of walled Jericho with trumpets. But how many of us stop to realize that our Savior's name is really Joshua?

We say His name in Greek today because the original English translators left it the way they found it in the Greek manuscripts—"Jesus." In Hebrew the name was "Yeshua" (Redeemer). Though it is the usual practice to render proper names just as they are found when translating an original, if we pronounce "Yeshua" (Jesus) in English we have "Joshua," and we suddenly see a beautiful Bible analogy (called a "type").

Joshua was the one who delivered his people to their promised land at the sound of the trumpet. Our Joshua will do the same for us!

The symbol of the trumpet urges us still further back, to the Book of Leviticus, where God established for His people the dramatic Feast of Trumpets (Leviticus 23:42). In Leviticus 23, God gave Moses a quick-reference guide to all the feasts which were to be established as "holy convocations" among the Jews for all time. The proper dates of each observance are given, as well as the important sacrifices and duties connected with each commemoration.

The feasts are described in other places in the Old Testament, but Leviticus 23 serves as a kind of handbook of the most vital elements of each feast. A believer could carry with him this one page of the Bible and he wouldn't miss any of these solemn convocations. God is practical.

The association between the trumpet of the Rapture and the trumpet of the Feast of Trumpets gives us an understanding of prophecy and redemption which are hard to grasp in any other way. In the feasts God made a kind of tapestry of future events, and in later actions He fulfilled these events.

The Rapture is the event which fulfills the Feast of Trumpets, as we shall see, and the position of this feast among the others tells us a great deal about our coming redemption.

The Feast of Trumpets comes fifth in the series of seven feasts, and it occurs on the first day of the seventh month (*Tishrei*), which falls in late August or September on our Julian calendar. The Jews call it *Rosh Hashanah* today—"the Head of the Months" —and they celebrate it as the beginning of the new year. They send new year's greetings on this day, though this tradition disagrees with the Jewish Torah (the first five books of the Bible). Leviticus 23:5 and Exodus 12 clearly establish Nisan, the month of Passover, as the first month of the year.

Many of the Jewish observances have been altered from their original requirements through the leavening of tradition and through the destruction of the second Temple in 70 A.D. The feasts are primarily oriented around sacrifices, and the Temple of God in Jerusalem was the only appropriate place to offer them (2 Chronicles 7:12). Because the sacrifices have not been possible for some 19 centuries, other kinds of observances have replaced them.

The ancient Jews went to considerable trouble to keep these feasts. A total of three pilgrimages to

Jerusalem were required each year during the three festival seasons of Passover, Pentecost, and Tabernacles. The first and third seasons take in three feasts each, as we will see, but the devout Jew couldn't get by with less than three trips each year to observe all seven feasts at the Temple.

We get a picture of the international atmosphere of the widely traveled Jews at their worship in Acts 2. This electrifying chapter, which describes the coming of the Holy Spirit, lists some 16 nations from which the Jews had come to keep the Feast of Pentecost. The gift of tongues was a necessity for sharing the gospel on that particular scene. Carelessly called "Pentecost One" by some Christians, this feast had actually been celebrated for over 1000 years by the hearty Jewish pilgrims!

But though the Jews were careful to observe their feasts, they tragically missed the fulfillments of these feasts in Christ. Let's look carefully at the seven feasts and their fulfillments, and we won't miss the Rapture when it comes!

## 1. THE FEAST OF PASSOVER
(Leviticus 23:5)

Passover was established during the tenth plague, in which Pharaoh was finally persuaded to let the Jewish people leave Egypt. God's avenging angel killed the firstborn in each Egyptian household, but he *passed over* the homes of the Jews. The Jews had been instructed to mark their door-posts with the blood of a lamb ("without blemish, a male . . ."— Exodus 12:5). The blood of the lamb would deliver them from slavery. It was their mark of redemption.

This principle is also dramatically true in Christianity. The blood of Christ, our Lamb, delivers us from slavery to sin. Paul refers to the Lord as "Christ our Passover" (1 Corinthians 5:7).

It is remarkable that the Jewish nation missed this fulfillment of their feast. John the Baptist tried valiantly to communicate this truth about Christ when he introduced Him. John did not say "Behold the *Son* of God" or "Behold the *Savior* of the world;" rather, he said pointedly "Behold *Lamb* of God, which taketh away the sin of the world" (John 1:29).

This must have held quite a bit of meaning for the Jews present with John as he baptized. But many later missed the point.

Significantly, the Lord was crucified exactly on Passover day, 14 Nisan. The night before, while Christ was celebrating the Passover meal with His disciples, He lifted the wine and said, "For this is my blood of the new testament [covenant], which is shed for many for the remission of sins."

Those Jews, the Lord's own disciples, surely understood the imagery there, but most Jews today continue to celebrate Passover in remembrance of the Exodus from Egypt. Though this was perfectly proper before the Messiah's coming, it is tragically inappropriate now that the feast has been fulfilled.

Passover, then, is the first of the feasts—the first one given and the first one fulfilled.

## 2. THE FEAST OF UNLEAVENED BREAD (Leviticus 23:6)

The seven-day Feast of Unleavened Bread begins on the day following Passover. Nisan, the first month (which contains the first three feasts), corresponds to late March or early April on our Julian calendar.

God commanded the Jews to eat only pure, unleavened bread during this week, for leaven symbolized sin and evil. As sin corrupts and permeates the human condition, so leaven corrupts and permeates bread dough.

The Apostle Paul developed this symbol further when he urged Christians to "purge out the old leaven" by purifying themselves (1 Corinthians 5:7).

The Jews today conduct a ceremony of ridding their homes of leaven in order to sanctify the dwellings for Passover. The father of the house hides bread crumbs and cookie particles on bookshelves and window sills, and the children come running to find them. When they discover the hidden leaven they shout for father. He comes with a feather and a wooden spoon, sweeping the crumbs into the spoon with the feather and ceremonially throwing them out the window.

The fulfillment of this Biblical "type" in Christ emphasizes the Lord's body. At His Passover table He took the unleavened bread and called it His body, even as He afterward referred to the wine as His blood. The bread makes an excellent symbol of His body: it is striped, pierced, and pure. Because of the way the unleavened bread is prepared (without fat or any rising agent), it bears stripes from the grill, and it must be pierced to cook through.

During the actual Passover meal, the Jews perform a unique ceremony with the unleavened bread. They place three pieces of it in one little stack. Then they take out the middle piece (the Son in the triune Godhead) and break it. ("This is my body, broken for you"). Next, they wrap the broken piece in white linen and hide it or bury it.

They bring this broken piece out again and eat it while drinking the third cup of wine, the "Cup of Redemption."

Incredibly, most Jews have failed to see the gospel in this ceremony repeated every year on the anniversary of Christ's crucifixion!

God performed the exact fulfillment of this ceremony with the unleavened Bread of Life, giving to all of us the Cup of Redemption.

## 3. THE FEAST OF FIRST FRUITS
### (Leviticus 23:10)

The feast of thanksgiving for a bountiful land occurs on Sunday ("the morrow after the Sabbath") during the Week of Unleavened Bread. The Israeli farmers were to bring the initial yield of their spring barley crop to Jerusalem, where a priest would wave these firstfruits before the House of the Lord.

This was most clearly fulfilled by Jesus, who was resurrected on the Sunday during the week of Unleavened Bread. Paul explains: "For as in Adam all die, even so in Christ shall all be made alive [resurrected]. But every man in his own order: *Christ for the firstfruits,* and afterwards they that are Christ's at His coming" (1 Corinthians 15:22, 23).

The Jewish leaders have failed to notice that Jesus was raised on the Sunday following Passover (or they have assumed that this is a fabrication of the New Testament intended to give the story credence to the Jews). Christians call this day "Easter" rather than Firstfruits and perhaps also miss the ultimate significance of this prophetic feast. It is not only that *Christ* was raised; we will *all* be raised, and so we celebrate! He was the firstfruits, but we will all follow in due time.

Again, however, this resurrection concerns only "they that are Christ's" (1 Corinthians 15:23).

The Jews do not celebrate Firstfruits at all anymore. Passover and Unleavened Bread have become one eight-day holiday, and the Sunday within this time span, despite all its Biblical significance, is not noted in any special way.

We might pause to realize a wonderful truth before going on to the remaining feasts. The feasts give us the Christian experience in chronological order.

First we had Passover, the blood sacrifice of Christ. Then we had Unleavened Bread, the celebration of His bodily sacrifice and the events connected with it during that final week of Christ's ministry. Then we had Firstfruits, celebrating both Christ's resurrection and ours to follow.

What would we expect next?

When Jesus was about to leave His disciples He promised them that they would not be left alone. The complex doctrines He had taught them would be refreshed in their memories, and their guidance through the difficult times ahead would be accomplished.

To do this the Lord was going to send the Comforter, the Holy Spirit.

## 4. THE FEAST OF PENTECOST
(Leviticus 23:16)

The spirit came as Christ had promised, at the Feast of Pentecost. Pentecost occurred 50 days after

Firstfruits on the Jewish calendar (usually in May or June). The disciples anxiously waited for this miracle. Christ had rejoined them for 40 days after His resurrection, but then He ascended to His Father. As he departed He instructed them to go to Jerusalem and await the fulfillment of His promise.

Sure enough, after ten days, when the Day of Pentecost was "fully come," the Holy Spirit came upon the worshipers at the Temple.

The deeper significance of this miracle is that it too fulfilled an Old Testament feast. The Spirit did not come on just any day, but on Pentecost, the beginning of the fullest harvest season. God's great harvest, the church age, was getting underway!

It is fascinating to realize that exactly 3000 people were saved on that remarkable day when the Spirit was given, while exactly 3000 people died on the day the Law was given on Mount Sinai! Truly, "the letter kills, but the Spirit gives life" (2 Corinthians 3:6)! Interestingly, in modern Judaism the Rabbis teach that Pentecost, or *Shevuoth* ("a week of weeks," or seven weeks) marks the day when Moses received the Law on the Mount. The Scriptures do indicate that this occurred in the third month (Exodus 19:1), after the exodus from Egypt (Nisan 14, of course), but the exact date is not given.

In the old observance of the feast, the priest was to wave two leavened loaves (Leviticus 23:17). These symbolize the Jew and Gentile together in heavenly places in Christ Jesus (Ephesians 2:6).

So Pentecost, the fourth feast, the "birthday" of both the Law and the Spirit, starts the church age, God's mighty harvest of human souls.

How does this period end? Because crops are planted in the spring and gathered in the fall, we should find a great harvest being brought in at the end of this age. And, true to our chronological schedule, the next feast symbolizes the Rapture of the believers!

## 5. THE FEAST OF TRUMPETS
### (Leviticus 23:24)

On the first day of the seventh month (late August or September on our calendar) was scheduled the Feast of Trumpets. This harvest-time feast is now clearly seen to represent the Rapture—the culmination of the church age, the final gathering of souls to God.

We now see the position of the Feast of Trumpets on God's calendar, and the reason why a trumpet sounds at the Rapture. God's placing of symbols is very beautiful indeed!

We will discuss the details of this thrilling feast in the next chapter and its full implications through the rest of the book, but we should point out here that in one sense the trumpet signals the beginning of the end. In unique and separate ways the trumpet will culminate God's plans for both the Jews and the church.

The Feast of Trumpets symbolizes "regathering" for both the church and the Jewish nation. The Rapture will culminate the redemption of the church, of course. But the trumpet will also regather the Jews to their land. Many years ago Isaiah heard God's trumpet (Isaiah 27:12,13) and foresaw a great homecoming of exiled Jews. More on that later.

The "beginning-of-the-end" aspect of the trumpet is expressed by the nature of the next feast, the solemn Day of Atonement. On this day the Jew made a special appeal for forgiveness, and by means of extraordinary effort he attempted to gain redemption.

## 6. THE DAY OF ATONEMENT
   (Leviticus 23:27)

This feast, following Trumpets by just ten days, represented the most solemn day on the ancient Jewish calendar—and it still does. On this day and this day alone, the High Priest of Israel, and he alone, would enter the Most Holy place of the sanctuary of the Lord. In this chamber where the Ark of the Covenant was placed, the High Priest would seek atonement (covering) for the sins of all Israel.

He would enter the first with the blood of a bull (with which he would atone for his own sin) and then with the blood of a goat (for the national sin of Israel). He would apply the blood to the mercy seat of the Ark.

It was a moment of such tension and drama that the Jewish people down through the ages feared that the High Priest could possibly die in the chamber. For this reason a rope was tied to his leg, so that if he didn't appear in due time he could be pulled out! No one except the High Priest was authorized to enter the Most Holy Place, but the dead body could not be permitted to defile the chamber.

Today the Jews have no Most Holy Place—in fact, no Temple at all—but they continue the tradition of Atonement with a long day of fasting and prayer. The tragedy is that, having spent the day in confession (*chatanu, chatanu*—"we have sinned, we have sinned"), the Jew gains no assurance of redemption at all.

The fulfillment of this feast for believers obviously lies in the finished work of Christ, through which everyone may claim permanent redemption. The chosen people will not be left out—the Day of Atonement will be fulfilled for "all Israel" on the coming occasion of the national atonement in the promised land.

Paul informs us that when the Deliverer (the Messiah, Christ) returns to Zion, "all Israel will be saved" (Romans 11:26). Zechariah proclaims a coming day when Israel will mourn in national repentance and will finally accept her Messiah: "They shall look upon Me, whom they have pierced" (Zechariah 12:10). It may well be that the entire Jewish nation will urgently recite the penitential message of Isaiah 53, confessing their tragic error of rejecting Jesus the Messiah when He came to die for their sins. At that time they will realize a true Day of Atonement. Then will be opened a "fountain of cleansing" for the Jews. (Zechariah 13:1).

This will occur, according to the Biblical context, when Jesus returns after the Tribulation period and establishes His kingdom on the earth. This follows the Rapture, of course, and is in keeping with our chronology.

All Jews will then experience the *Christian* Day of Atonement—the day on which the believer receives Christ and stands before his Creator as a forgiven man.

## 7. THE FEAST OF TABERNACLES
(Leviticus 23:34)

We would expect by this time, seeing the logic of the chronological order of the feasts, for the final feast to symbolize the Millennium, that 1000-year rule of Christ on earth which follows the other events we have discussed so far. And it does indeed.

The Feast of Tabernacles takes us back to the times of the Israelites in the wilderness (Leviticus 23:42, 43), when they lived in makeshift shelters or "booths." This is the feast of *Succoth* (tabernacles), in which the Almighty wished the Jews to remember how He took care of them in inhospitable surroundings. This feast also looks forward to the coming kingdom as pictured by Zechariah (14:16-19).

The orthodox Jews believe in the Messianic implications of the Feast of Tabernacles. They build little shelters from which hang fruit and nuts, and some actually sleep in the "tabernacles" for the duration of the eight-day feast. They feel that this feast is a harbinger of the peace and rest that will come to Israel and the world in the "days of Messiah," when "every man will dwell under his own vine and fig tree." (Micah 4:4).

This is fulfilled in the Christian believer, of course. This feast will clearly be fulfilled during Christ's coming reign on earth, when everyone "shall even go up from year to year to worship the King, the Lord of Hosts, and to keep the Feast of Tabernacles (Zechariah 14:16). The prophet adds a bit of admonishment to the nations, noting that those who fail to get to Jerusalem during the Feast of Tabernacles will have no rain. Egypt is singled out an an example of those who might omit this feast in the coming Kingdom.

That time will see quite a different earthly society from what we see today. The Christian nation of Isreal will finally take its place as the "head of the nations," and the church, the Bride of Christ, will reign with the Lord. At that time the meek will truly have "inherited the earth" (Matthew 5:5). In those days "the knowledge of the Lord will cover the earth as the waters cover the sea" (Isaiah 11:9).

## OUR POSITION ON THE TIMETABLE

There were no more feasts in the Law, and no need for any more. God gave these symbolic feasts for the entire Christian chronology in sequential order. The feasts take us from Christ to Christ—from His sacrifice (Passover) to His reign (Tabernacles); from the Lamb to the Lion.

The very spacing of the feasts throughout the year displays God's redemptive program for us. The first three feasts come in rapid succession (Passover, Unleavened Bread, and Firstfruits), showing the sacrifice, burial, and resurrection of Christ. Then there is a pause until the Holy Spirit comes (Pentecost). Then follows an extended pause for the church age (the harvest). Then the Rapture, the granting of atonement, and the establishment of the kingdom (Trumpets, Atonement, and Tabernacles) come again in rapid succession to finish the timetable.

In a further divine symbol, God illustrates His design of the seven-day week—six feasts work, the seventh feast rest.

Where are *we* on this timetable of God?

Obviously, we stand somewhere between the coming of the Spirit and the Rapture, in that long summer between Pentecost and Tabernacles.

Jesus Himself alluded to our position in the sequence of feasts when He admonished us to look to the harvest period: "Lift up your eyes, and look on the fields, for they are white already to harvest" (John 4:35).

Many Bible students believe that the harvest is almost over. The signs of "the end" as given in various Scriptural teachings, notably those of Jesus in Matthew 24, seem to be upon us today. It is a mistake to try to "schedule" the Rapture, to "pick a day." On the other hand, we would be remiss to fail to notice the signs of our times, or that the fields lie white and ready to harvest.

The Pentecostal harvest goes on, with the laborers working the fields and the unbelievers moving the world toward its ultimate tribulation. As the first four feasts were each fulfilled according to their special symbols, so will be the last three. As suddenly as the Spirit came to the Jews at that dramatic Pentecost after the Lord's ascension, just as suddenly will Jesus return for His own.

At the sound of the trumpet.

# Chapter 3

# THE TRUMPET
# AND THE EXILED
# CHURCH

*Alexei nearly burst into tears of fear as the KGB man passed within a few feet of his hiding place.*

*It was a very dark night, and the alley afforded maximum protection to the fugitive Christian as he huddled between the garbage cans. Had the policeman seen him it would have been all over. His now-useless work permit lay folded in his pocket, canceled some three weeks earlier, and now Alexei was a wanted man. His terror of the Gulag Archipelago, the prison system of the government, knew no bounds; he had a genuine fear for the horror that awaited Christians captured as "enemies of the state."*

*His own "crime" had been simple enough; he had quoted Christ during a philosophical discussion. It was a factory workers' meeting, and a point had* come up about the relationship of servants and masters. Without thinking, he had supplied the Lord's views, which were quite pertinent and reasonable, he thought. He saw no harm in sharing, as philosophy, the information he had gotten from his tattered, hand-copied Bible. He had felt a coldness in the room at his remarks, but he never suspected that his work permit would be affected. That was a catastrophe.

Without a work permit he had no right to exist. As a "non-worker" he simply did not have a place in the state, and the state, he well knew, would react accordingly. He would be arrested on a charge like vagrancy and conceivably accused of anything from disturbing the peace to high treason. The particular charges wouldn't matter; he knew that he would be incarcerated in the horrible prisons of endless labor and slow starvation. The state would discard him like a piece of rubbish.

He would not be accused of "Christianity." The state had not honored belief in the Lord Jesus with the status of being an actual crime. But they would fine a crime to suit his case; that would be no problem. And he would confess to it, he knew. He had talked to too many others who had been through the secret police interrogations to have any delusions about resisting their methods.

There was the old man in the church in the woods, who was called simply "Elder." (The church didn't use real names for fear of infiltration by the KGB). The old man prayed daily for the Rapture; his body had been so broken in the prisons that he cried out each day for a new one. He had never renounced his faith despite fifteen years of hard labor, and his guards had made a game of seeing how much they could torture him and still prolong his life. They had broken his flesh, but not his spirit. He still prayed "Come Lord Jesus" with a joyful gleam in his sightless eyes.

Alexei moved through the darkened streets on the outskirts of Moscow, traveling cautiously from tree to tree. It was still several miles to the church in the woods, but the fellowship there would quiet his fear. He had to make it!

He was eager to be with the other true believers and to hear their reports of the activities of the secret churches in China, Eastern Europe, and the rest of Russia. These stories always bolstered his faith, and at a time like this, when he had been discovered as a Christian, he needed his brothers and sisters more than ever. How he loved them, these enemies of the "worker's Paradise"—these reactionary holdouts against the "purity" of the state atheism! How proud he was to be fighting the good fight! How he longed to be with the Lord, who would say, "Well done, good and faithful servant!"

Alexei's mind wondered to the stories about Christianity in the Western World—printed Bibles, open churches, the gospel freely proclaimed. He didn't know what to make of these rumors. Could they actually be true? He had never known "free Christianity," and these stories often had the ring of mere wishful thinking. In any case, the West was inaccessible; the borders were closed. Thank God the Lord had not forgotten this part of the world. Thank God all Christians were eventually to meet at the same Place!

All that Alexei knew for sure was that the church didn't belong in this world. This was exile in the truest sense of the word, and he well knew that no *earthly society, controlled by Satan as they all were, truly welcomed the Christian church. And that had always been the way it was, all through the history of the Christian church.*

*In the distance Alexei spotted a lantern light flickering through the trees. He would be with his own in just a few minutes. He was well away from the city now and could walk upright. The police wouldn't bother to pursue him this far away from their normal jurisdiction.*

*He came to the first worshipers at the edge of the group and embraced them in his gladness. They looked at his face, drawn in fear but shining all the same with the presence of the Spirit.*

*"Maranatha!" they proclaimed. "The Lord is coming!"*

Back in the first century, the announcement that there was to be a "church" was the biggest spiritual news to hit the world in 2000 years.

That God had chosen a specific people, Israel, everybody knew. That much had been clear from the time of Abraham, about 2000 B.C. But the news that God was now to begin selecting a *second* chosen people was a real bombshell.

Today, after some 2000 years of church history since the time of Christ, we are quite used to the concept of the church, but we must appreciate the fact that not the merest hint of it was given in the Old Testament. Only God could anticipate, in the days of the prophets and the temple, that there would someday be a church and a church age. The prophets knew well enough that the Messiah would come to earth, suffer and die, rise from the dead, ascend into heaven, and eventually return in the clouds in judgment to establish His kingdom on earth. That much was clear in the sayings of the prophets and the reckonings of such men as David and Moses.

But only God knew about the church and its lengthy age.

Moses and Isaiah never knew that a long period of time would separate the two comings of Christ. Ezekiel and Zechariah, with all of their remarkable foresight, never dreamed that a new kind of humanity would be formed during the interadvent time. Even John the Baptist was not aware of the coming church age or its implications of a new people of God.

The Lord Jesus Himself was the first Person to allude to the church, in a conversation with His disciples. Realizing that false teachings about the Messiah were prevalent, Jesus asked His followers, "Whom do men say that I, the Son of Man, am?" He received a variety of answers to this query, ranging from a restored John the Baptist to certain of the prophets. But the astute Peter was able to answer correctly, "Thou art the Christ, the Son of the living God" (Matthew 16:16).

The Lord praised Peter for this insight, since ". . . flesh and blood hath not revealed it to thee, but my Father which is in heaven." Then Christ continued, "And I say also unto thee that thou are Peter, and upon this rock I will build my church . . ." (Matthew 16:17, 18).

We often use the term "church" to denote the building where Christians worship, but actually the word refers to the people themselves; it is taken from the Greek *ekklesia*, which means "called out ones." Christians are those people called out from among all the world's people to believe in Jesus Christ and to attach themselves to Him as Lord and Savior.

The Lord did not define or explain the meaning of the church during His earthly ministry, but Paul writes, ". . . how that by revelation He made known unto me the mystery . . . which in other ages was not made known unto the sons of men, as it is now revealed unto his holy apostles and prophets by the Spirit; that the Gentiles should be fellowheirs, and of the same body, and partakers of his promise in Christ by the gospel" (Ephesians 3:3,5,6).

Paul's stress is on the new privileges of the Gentiles, since only the Jews had previously been God's chosen people. The church is composed of both Jewish and Gentile believers in the Lord Jesus, with both groups being "fellowheirs" to His great promises. They become "one body" or "one new man" in Christ.

This was an entirely new picture of spiritual things, for previously there had been only two kinds of people in the world—Jews and Gentiles. Now, however, there are three kinds—unsaved Jews, unsaved Gentiles, and the church. Paul admonishes believers to "give none offence, neither to Jews, nor to the Gentiles, nor to the church of God" (1 Corinthians 10:32).

God's two chosen peoples, the Jews and the church, were chosen for different purposes and have different destinies. Israel, the Jewish people, were chosen to be God's separate nation upon the earth. They were given an earthly law (the Torah), an earthly capital (Jerusalem), and an earthly day of rest (the Sabbath). The church (including saved

Jews, of course) was chosen to represent Christ, her heavenly Head, to testify to the grace and good news of the crucified and risen Savior and to demonstrate by her love of all men the tremendous love of God.

To be a part of Israel was good; one could partake in a national convenantal relationship with God. But to be a part of the church is even better; a Christian is a child of God and has personal, eternal salvation.

One might have thought that the church, God's masterpiece on earth, would have enjoyed immediate and sustained success, but there were problems right from the beginning. The Lord had warned about the "tares" or weeds that would grow among the good wheat (Matthew 13:38, 39) and Paul spoke of the wolves who would enter and try to devour the sheep (Acts 20:29). The church was hardly underway when the substance of these warnings was come to pass.

It very quickly became apparent that it was going to be difficult to keep the church pure. People would come along who only pretended to follow Christ, and they would attempt to disrupt the movement. All sorts of theological ideas which differed from the pure truth of Scripture began to permeate the church and the believers began to stumble in many ways. The Lord's evaluation of the original churches as found in the beginning chapters of the Book of Revelation provides a picture of many false starts and complex problems among the called-out people of God. Right from the beginning the church faced Satanic opposition from the outside as well as error and disruption from within.

And so it has been for 19 centuries. The church has always had a difficult existence in the world, for the world has never had a clear understanding of what the church is all about and what it's doing here in the first place. Away from its ultimate home in heaven the church has been in exile, in a sense, traveling with a predominately unbelieving world through many hostile periods. Since the time of Christ, the Christians have been "strangers and pilgrims" on the earth, struggling to be the ambassadors of Christ to a cynical and adverse race of men.

The church, like the Jews, has faced persecution in the world from all sides—even from societies claiming falsely to be the true church. The unsaved Jews have never understood the true "Jewishness" of the church—that their own Jesus is the promised Messiah or that through Him believing Gentiles can be heirs of father Abraham. Jewish Christians, historically and in our present time, have experienced ostracism by their unbelieving Jewish friends and even by their own families. Paul likens the situation to the taunting of Isaac who was "born after the Spirit," by Ishmael, who was "born after the flesh" (Galatians 4:28, 29).

The Gentiles have also been hostile to the church from its very beginning and down through the ages. Thousands of believers have perished at the hands of the Romans, who crucified the Christians and fed them to the lions. In the infamous Inquisition, true believers were tortured and burned, ostensibly for their lack of allegiance to the "church." Our own century has seen dictators trying to wipe out all witness for Christ, for true Christianity never bows to totalitarianism. Hitler tried to destroy the church or at least to make it conform to the odious Nazi position. In the Communistic societies (which control more than a third of the human race at present), Christians are systematically hunted down, harassed, imprisoned, tortured, and destroyed. The Scriptures are forbidden, or worse, they suffer a contolled "distribution" by the government. Instruction in Christianity is a crime.

Even in the free world today, where freedom of worship was initially carved out at great cost, the true body of Christ faces much resentment and opposition. The apostate church, always on the job of defeating the true believers, has popularized false teachings and unscriptural practices and has mounted an enormous ecumenical movement. Satanic deception continues and the church struggles onward.

Obviously it has been a rough sojourn for the church in this world. The church is simply not at home here, and it won't be until the world is changed through the coming leadership of the Lord Himself. The church belongs to heaven, not earth, and it longs for that promised voyage to come at the sound of the trumpet. Whether through death or through the Rapture, the individual Christian lives in great expectation of being delivered from a basically unworkable and unhappy situation on earth.

Our task here will soon be done, or at least called off. The witnessing which has continued in the face of all the wandering, struggling, and persecution will be concluded soon, at the pleasure of the Lord, who has given the world extraordinary time and opportunity to come to Him. The ordeal of the coming Tribulation and judgment will become the fate of the world as the church goes home.

We will enjoy the presence of the Lord Jesus forever. While He is in heaven we will be with Him there. When He returns to earth to establish His kingdom, we will be with Him there too. When the new heaven, the new earth, and the New Jerusalem are ready, we will still be with our Savior. Throughout all eternity—forever—we will luxuriate in the very presence of the Lord Jesus Christ.

It has been worth it! Let the Rapture trumpet sound; we're ready to go home!

# Chapter 4

# THE TRUMPET
# AND THE
# WANDERING JEWS

*They looked into each others' totally defeated faces. None of them knew whether he would be alive the next day.*

*Some of them didn't care anymore.*

*The young blond guards would come around later that day in their snappy Nazi uniforms and select a dozen or so Jews from the barracks. No one understood how the selections were made—only that those selected would never be seen again. The way of death at Auschwitz Concentration Camp was utterly inexplicable, though it seemed that a certain percentage of those living must die each day, presumably until there were none left.*

*Some theorized that weakness or illness decided the issue—that the guards chose those who appeared to be dying already. So some of the inmates tried to* adopt a healthy appearance and even a smiling, positive attitude. But others, craving death and an end to the steady starvation, and hating the insult of being considered one of the expendable "inferior" race, came forward and volunteered for the selection.

Sometimes the guards would choose the sick and sometimes the healthy; sometimes the smiling and sometimes the gaunt-faced. Sometimes the young men and sometimes the old; a few from this barracks and a few from that.

Somehow the guards did not seem unkind or murderous in their intentions. It was as though they were walking through a dog kennel selecting sick animals to be exterminated. The guards were matter-of-fact; they understood something that completely escaped the inmates—that the inmates were "subhumans"—Jews.

So they chose people to go to the gas chambers across the compound—and then to the ovens near the gas chambers. And those in the barracks could smell the stench and speculate about the next visit of the guards.

Women were chosen, as well as little children. Those left behind each day—those not chosen—knew only that their lives were temporarily spared by the limited efficiency of the death machines. After all, there was only so much flesh that the oven could dispose of in a single day! How many people could share the same breath of gas before it lost its potency? What was the optimum ratio of exterminated children to exterminated adults, considering the proportions of the society to be exterminated versus the amount of space consumed by each size of corpse?

*The younger women had special fears, but their overlords were so convinced of their inferior racial characteristics that by and large rape was considered beneath the preferences of the black-booted Aryans. It happened sometimes, of course, but under the circumstances who could care?*

*"Chosen people," reflected Joseph bitterly as he sat against the wall of the barracks. They were certainly being "chosen." He looked at the shelves that lined the walls, where the sick and dying were stacked like shoe boxes. Occasionally one of these would cheat the system; when the guard would prod him to come along he would already be dead. The guard would frown and mutter something to his assistant, and a trip straight to the ovens, without the usual stop at the gas chambers, would have to be arranged. The guard would probably feel that he'd made a mistake; he should have stopped at that shelf the day before.*

*How many thousands had gone already? Joseph wondered.*

*But there was one glimmer of hope. New prisoners coming in had given reports of trouble for the Nazis on the outside. Apparently the battles were going very hard for the Third Reich in these last days of 1944, and they had been losing a lot of ground. There might come a time when the Germans would have to fall back from Auschwitz. The ovens were running steadily at full capacity, of course, but the Jews were numerous and the Germans' time might be limited. Perhaps the guards would be unable to kill every last one of the prisoners.*

*And so Joseph and a number of the other younger surviving men made a solemn pact. Every attempt at* escape would be tried, however hopeless, and every attempt at survival. They would not lie down and succumb to disease or despair. They would not volunteer for the ovens, no matter how intense the agony.

Instead, they would think about Israel day and night, without ceasing. And their solemn agreement was that any of them who survived or escaped would go to Israel, to the Promised Land. Nothing would stop them, not friends nor family, not the entire Second World War, wherever it might be or however ferocious. If they had to crawl there on their knees, they would go to Israel. If only one man survived of their group, he would go to Israel by himself.

And there a stand would be made. The Jew would hold fast there, on his own land. And no power on earth would move the Jew again!

This was the last extermination of the Jews, they swore. This was the last time the Chosen People would be treated as "inferior." Let the maniacs come as they may, whether "Aryans" or some other super race—they would never kill the Jew so easily again.

It was hard to find volunteers for resistance among the utterly vanquished personalities of their little death row. Some of their fellow inmates had become partially convinced that they actually were inferior—this seemed to be the only way they could understand the horrors around them. Some had the delusion that if they even thought about some kind of brighter future the guards would somehow know and they would be selected. But Joseph and his dwindling group constantly sought men who would join them in their rather pitiful but heartfelt vows.

One day an aged Rabbi found himself in Ausch-

*witz and gave his blessing to these courageous men, calling them Maccabees after the heroic Jewish free-dom-fighters of the ancient era of Antiochus. The Rabbi joined their cause, promising, "If God brings me out of here alive, they'll see just how old and fee-ble I am in Israel!"*

*The Rabbi was a wonderful tonic to the group. He explained that they had every right to Israel—that God had in fact promised it to them and that the prophets had said that they would someday re-turn to it. He explained that the Naizs, with all of their expertise at annihilating the Jews, were hardly the first to try it, and he told them the heartbreaking history of the persecution of the Jews. He pointed out that the Scriptures said clearly that this disper-sion would someday be finished—that the exile of the Jews would be over. He told them that their wandering though seemingly endless, would some-day have an end. Palestine, he said, was theirs!*

*As hope filtered in from the outside their group gained membership and strength. They knew each other at a glance—the ones with hope in their eyes—and their faith never wavered.*

*"Someday," Joseph prayed constantly, "we will go home. Someday Jews in their own land will remem-ber these miserable millions crushed under the heels of the Jew-haters. God, make me one of them—one of the future Israelis! I promise to keep the land and to love it, to fight off the pagan and to plant the fields again. I promise to represent properly to the world what a Jew is—a chosen one of God, a unique and precious soul in the world.*

*"O God, if it is my lot to die here, then let Israel remember me and my brothers and sisters. Let them not forget how we suffered—what they did to us*

*here. Let them remember us when the Gentile comes, because he surely will, as he always has. Let them stand against the entire world if necessary, Eternal One, in memory of us and in honor of Israel. Let the Jew live!"*

The poignant Tevye, hero of "Fiddler on the Roof," is very frank with God in his prayers. He looks upward with a sigh one day and tells his Maker, "I know we Jews are your chosen people, but why don't you choose somebody else for awhile?"

Tevye is part of the Diaspora, that cruel and seemingly endless dispersion of God's chosen people over the whole earth for some 2000 years. They began to leave their promised land in 70 A.D., when the heartless Titus sent the crack tenth legion of Rome against the holy Temple.

Over a million Jewish people died in that bloodbath of the first century, and in a very real way the chosen people have never recovered. The majority still remain exiled from Israel. They have yet to return after 19 centuries.

But they *will* return, as we have seen, when that

great Biblical symbol of deliverance sounds—the trumpet of God.

In order to understand this fully we should note a certain worship ceremony connected with the Old Testament Feast of Trumpets. The Jews were called to their worship on that occasion by a literal blowing of the *shofar*—the ram's horn—which was the trumpet of Biblical times. (At the Rapture we are likely to hear this original sound, with a hunting horn quality, rather than the modern brassy modern trumpet.)

It happened this way: The Jews left Jerusalem following the Feast of Pentecost in the Spring, and they spent the summer harvesting wheat in the land. Some three months would pass until the time of Trumpets—the first day of the seventh month on their calendar, or around the beginning of September on ours. When the harvest was complete they would make their pilgrimage to Jerusalem. There the High Priest would stand on the high peak of the southwestern corner of the Temple mount and sound the trumpet, calling the nation together for the holy feast. The people would gather in the Temple at the sound of the trumpet to commemorate the holiday.

Isaiah employed this imagery in his clear-eyed forecast of the dramatic regathering of the exiles in the end times:

> And it shall come to pass in that day, that the great trumpet shall be blown, and they shall come which were ready to perish. . . .
>
> —Isaiah 27:13

So the trumpet is the signal for the regathering and deliverance—for homecoming. And it pertains, obviously, to all of God's children.

But this brings up a tricky point. It's not as easy as it once was to identify "God's children."

In the Old Testament things were very clear on this, and everyone knew who was who in God's sight. There were Jews and there were the others; the Jews belonged to God and that's all there was to that. From Abraham to Christ the Almighty carefully nurtured His own people, the Jews, blessing and disciplining them as God's only children. This went on for 2000 alternately happy and tragic years.

But with the advent of the Messiah God began calling out people from among the other nations. The indefatigable Apostle Peter testified to the devout Gentile Cornelius, and his household became followers of the Messiah (Acts 10). The church, then entirely Jewish, realized the validity of these conversions and adopted an unheard-of resolution:

> Then hath God also to the Gentiles granted repentance unto life.
>
> —Acts 11:18

God was about to create, as it were, another chosen people.

This new group came enthusiastically out of all nations. They were called the church (Greek *ekklesia,* the called-out ones). And they took their gift of salvation very seriously, growing into a powerful world body, always awaiting their promised kingdom to come.

We are now, of course, living in this church age, and the world contains two kinds of chosen people. The Jews are still chosen, of course; God's covenants with them are immutable, promised for-

RAPTURED

ever. And the church is chosen, too.

This explains the phenomenon of people heading in two different directions at the sound of the trumpet. The two homecoming groups have different homes; the Christians go immediately to be with the Lord, and the Jews regather to Israel. (The living Jews will ultimately be saved, as we have seen— Romans 11:26—after the Tribulation period at the Lord's second coming.)

Looking ahead speculatively, it seems very logical that the Jews will want to return to Israel when the Rapture occurs. The world will have changed, in the twinkling of an eye, into a place where no true believers are found. Atheists have been notoriously tough on the Jews (for example, Nazis and Communists) because the Jews at all times and in all circumstances insist on pursuing their own peculiar worship practices. The society of the Antichrist will provide little comfort to this persecuted people, and they will survive best by banding together in their ancient homeland. There they will have their Temple of God, the Tribulation Temple to be built in the end times, and freedom of worship, at least until the Antichrist takes over the Temple.

The whole world will follow them to Israel, of course, where the horrible carnage of Armageddon will take place, but at least at the time of the trumpet, the Rapture, Israel will represent an island of safety for the Jews.

Thus Isaiah's subtle observation of the regathering at the sound of the trumpet would be fulfilled.

When the church was initially created it raised a pointed question that is still being asked in some sectors. Since God was choosing a new people—those Jews and Gentiles who believe in Christ—what would happen with the old chosen people? Because comparatively few Jews have come to Christ during the church age, some people have assumed that God has switched peoples.

This age-old question must have been going the rounds in the church at the time of Paul, because he dealt with it in his Letter to the Romans. "Hath God cast away His people?" asked the Apostle rhetorically (Romans 11:1).

He answers the question most emphatically: "God forbid!" (*mē genoito*). Stronger language would not be possible in Scripture. Paul goes on to emphasize, "For I also am an Israelite," offering himself as living proof that God had certainly not forgotten His original children.

But as the church went on, the Jews were pretty well forgotten by men, until only a few of the Israelites today belong to Christ. Not many Jews will be heading upward at the Rapture, compared to those heading back to Israel.

The past 1000 years have not really been happy ones for either of God's chosen peoples, by and large. Neither group is truly at home in the world, since both have a more meaningful destination and a better ultimate home. The true church, like the original chosen people, has suffered in this age. And the Jews have been outcasts even in their homes away from home.

The true church has its citizenship in heaven, that "kingdom not of this world" which is ruled by Christ. We in the true church are described in Scripture as "strangers and pilgrims" in this "vale of tears." Truly the believers in Christ have been persecuted, just as the Jews were, by governments, by religions, and even by so-called church institutions.

The infamous Inquisitions dealt as severely with Christians who would not renounce their true faith as with the detested children of Israel.

Looking at the world as a whole today, there are still very few places where a believer in Christ can worship and proclaim the good news to his neighbors. We Americans somtimes lose sight of the fact that religious freedom is a rare privilege, and that vast areas of the world today are under atheistic governmental control and are utterly hostile to faith in Christ.

Even when we die and our souls go to be with the Lord, we will not yet truly be home. Heaven is now filled with the souls of those who died in faith, who await their future eternal bodies. At the Rapture the full metamorphosis will finally be made—souls will be joined to eternal, victorious, sinless bodies—and we of God's church will at last be home. Until then we just have to make the best of this earthly sojourn, with God's help.

Similarly, the Jews have been homeless throughout the church age, and their story is even more tragic. The church is composed of people who all individually *choose* to be true believers. But each Jew is *born* to his miserable lot in this world; he has no choice in the matter.

The Jewish dispersion began with slavery in the first century, and it hasn't changed much to date. Wherever Abraham's descendants went they were considered second-class citizens and scapegoats for every negative development in their adopted homeland. If a plague came it was blamed on the Jews; if money was short the Jews must have taken it. The ugliest accusation against the chosen people was that of child murder; it was said that Jews killed Gentile children to use their blood in their worship.

The story of the wandering Jew (after whom we've named a houseplant because of its unpredictable spreading growth) has been repeated around the world. The Jews would get a moment's rest in some successful civilization, but then they would have to run for it at the first sign of anti-Semitism. They would settle down uneasily in an adjacent country, only to have to pack and move overnight again. A tradition eventually developed as part of the Passover worship: the Jews would wear their hats over their skullcaps in order to be ready to travel at a moment's notice.

When they prospered for a while in some new land, the Jews would regroup, establish their synagogues and their home worship, and keep the grand traditions alive. Young people, would marry and raise families and their children, normally not permitted to practice the professions, would go into some business.

But then the economic, political, or religious conditions would change in the hosting country, and the chosen people would begin to hear "dirty Jew" or "ritual murder," and they would get their ever-ready traveling gear together quickly again. It wasn't that they would run for it at the first sign of trouble. They actually put up with incredibly insulting and dangerous conditions time and again. In England in the Middle Ages they were obliged to wear big yellow Stars of David on their coats so that all might know when the inferiors passed on the streets. They were considered dirty, sneaky, and avaricious, and even if they wished to consider the gospel they were not permitted entrance to any Christian church (a far cry from the original New Testament Jewish mission to the Gentiles!).

The peerless Nazis finally came up with their "final solution to the Jewish problem," pronouncing the suffering chosen people vermin and proceeding to exterminate them like roaches or rats.

Careful readers of the Old Testament realized that God had warned of such things (Deuteronomy 28:63-68, for example), but the whole world became sympathetic at last when the results of the concentration camps were seen. Feeling a tinge of guilt, the world decided that the Jews might have a land after all, and Israel was returned to them. God had also spoken of this restoration (for example, in Ezekiel 37:1-11), but it was anything but peaceful. At the time of this writing the pagan has pursued the Jew to the holy land once again, and the worldly future of the children of Israel remains in doubt.

This restoration of the holy land doesn't really describe the ultimate regathering of the Jews seen by Isaiah. Actually there are more Jewish people in New York City than in all of Israel, and the chosen people remain primarily in the dispersion. Some ten million Jews are still exiles, at this writing, with less than three million living in Israel. The U.S. has six million, three million are trying to leave the USSR, and the rest are widely scattered all over the world.

In America, virtually a land of refugees of all kinds from its beginning, the Jew has survived better than ever before. But there are present fears that the oil situation and the Mideast powder keg could easily cause an anti-Jewish response among the Gentile Americans, and some coldhearted spokesmen have already suggested forsaking Israel in favor of the Arabs and their oil. Moral perceptions are dulled by pinches in the pagan pocketbook!

The weight of history bears against the Jews, even in America. There is a likelihood of real persecution here, and Rabbi Meyer Kahane of the Jewish Defense League has recently published the foresighted book *Time to Go Home.* The Rabbi warns of the impending repetition of the tragic history of the chosen people.

The Rabbi may have hit on a profound truth, but the real time to go home for the Jews was specified by the prophets, as we have seen. They will go home at the Rapture, when they hear the trumpet of God.

In a larger sense the Jews will be going home to God's home on earth when they return to the Promised Land. Jesus will set up His kingly rule in Jerusalem after the Tribulation period (Zechariah 14:16), and Israel will take its promised place at the head of the nations (Deuteronomy 28:13). The Jews still living when Jesus returns will all be saved, as we have seen, and Zechariah draws a dramatic picture of the salvation of the world's first Christian nation, Israel (Zechariah 13). The Jews will at last utter the password to the kingdom, "Blessed is He who comes in the name of the Lord" (see Matthew 23:37-39).

The Jew today, then, has two alternatives. He can receive his Messiah now and join him at the sound of the trumpet, or he can try to survive until Armageddon, retreating to Israel at the sound of the trumpet and awaiting the Lord there in the midst of the bloodshed. If he dies or is killed between now and the day of the second coming he is a permanently dead man, no different than any pagan who died without the Lord.

At the risk of sounding like life insurance salesmen, we strongly recommend the Lord as things stand now!

Let's recap all that we have said about the trumpet: it will sound for both chosen peoples. The church, including all saved Jews, will meet the Lord in the air in the Rapture, and their troubles will be over. The unsaved Jews will regather in Israel and try to hang on while the Antichrist masterminds the Tribulation period, leading the world to final disaster. The Lord will return to end the Battle of Armageddon; otherwise "there would be no flesh saved" (Matthew 24:22). The surviving Jews will receive their Messiah and the kingdom will get underway for all believers. (See the authors' books *The Coming Russian Invasion of Israel* and *Satan in the Sanctuary* for a more complete discussion of the details of the end times regarding the Jews and the church.)

We would be remiss, in this book about the Rapture, to fail to specify the alternative for the unbelievers. Only the church is going up at the Rapture, so the vast majority of the world (as things look now) is staying.

Every Christian who is witnessing for the Lord would do well to understand what his unbelieving friends and neighbors face in the upcoming godless world. Sometimes a word to the wise is enough to persuade a person into a policy change, and more than a few souls have been saved by a clear presentation of the deadly alternative.

Moreover, the authors feel that all Christian books should clearly set down the "history of the future" in these times so that future unbelievers may study them in the light of the tribulations they will be experiencing. Hopefully a dear brother or sister in the hard times to come will say, "Those fellows were right; it's all happening right here and now! I'd better make my peace with God at once!"

We Christians are going to meet the Lord, but we're not going to take our books with us. Our Bibles, it stands to reason, will remain, along with our books about the faith. They will be here on earth to read at the time the Antichrist is here promoting his atheistic doctrines. Unbelievers can still be saved then, and they'll need some information, to say the least.

Our next chapter will have to be an unhappy one, for our world will come to a sad and dramatic end.

Here, for your information, and for those who may desperately need this knowledge in the times to come, is the Great Tribulation, starring the Antichrist, and the kingdom to come, starring the real Christ.

# Chapter 5

# ISRAEL IN AGONY

*Seven years of bad luck!*

*That was all he could think of as he plunged headlong through the rocky Kidron Valley, running for his life.*

*It had been seven steady years of terror, of running, of hiding. That he was still alive was downright surprising, but was this living?*

*It had started back in the States, he remembered, when he and the rest of the synagogue officers had decided that a retreat to Israel was the only thing left to do. The persecution of the Jews had developed slowly back then, as it had in Germany in the thirties. First there were the problems with the civic clubs, the social organizations, and so forth—it had become harder and harder for a Jew to get membership. He and his friends had started up their own or-*

*ganizations where the Jews could fellowship without feeling like they were intruding.*

*But then came the problems of new zoning laws, mysterious people buying up neighboring real estate, and the inevitable Arab financiers behind the transactions. Trouble with the banks started too, and notes were called in without warning. Then it was troubles in the schools. First there were exams on Jewish holy days, seemingly on purpose; then special school taxes for Jews, special social security forms, special this and special that. He and his associates recognized the historic patterns—it would only be a matter of time until the smashing of the store windows, the burning of the synagogues, and the beatings in the streets. They decided to run for it.*

*But where should they run? He bitterly remembered the arrival in Israel, amidst general panic and a hopeless overload of immigrants from so many lands. He could certainly forgive his brothers in Israel. They just weren't ready for the millions who descended on the little citadel of Judaism in the Middle East. But he would never forgive the Russians.*

*He was in Israel barely a month, unable to speak the language, unable to settle his family, unable to find employment as yet, when the Russians perpetrated their cowardly invasion. They got what was coming to them, he felt. If they weren't smart enough to realize that Israel was capable of repelling a land invasion, even from Russian and her allies, they deserved what they got. He was not clear on how Israel had won that "instant war," but there was talk of some secret nuclear weapons that completely surprised and decimated the invading enemy. Some people credited "divine retribution." The world then developed a healthy new respect for Israel, especially when the new Leader stepped forward with his guarantees of peace for the Middle East.*

*He had felt drawn to the Leader at once after those fearful days of the invasion. Here was a man who talked sense, at least at the beginning. Every country in the world subscribed to his lofty ideals of a one-world community with common goals, common money, and common principles of peace for all men.*

*But he bitterly remembered, too, how the Leader had seemingly let his power go to his head. Nobody had been asking for any religious slant to the new regime, but the Leader had begun to sound more and more like some kind of god on earth, dictating not only political and economic policies to the nations, but moral and spiritual values as well. In his own Jewishness something seemed to revolt against the Leader at that point; he just didn't like that quasi-religious air in the world government.*

*The new Temple of Jerusalem had been a one-of-a-kind achievement for Israel, he remembered, and he had gone to the dedication with the millions who assembled in Jerusalem on that great day. The Leader had sent his congratulations and hailed the Temple as a crowning glory of the new system of world peace.*

*But only 3½ years later he had disappointed the Jews terribly right in the Temple building. He had tried to take over the Temple and make it his headquarters! One could take his claims of being God with a grain of salt—lots of leaders develop egocentric tendencies as their careers go on. But the idea of the secular world government operating from the Jerusalem Temple had been too much for the Israe-*

*lis, and they withdrew their support from their for-mer mentor.*

*That's when all this trouble seemed to begin. That's when the newspapers started to fill with anti-Israeli sentiments from the rest of the nations, and editorials began to appear about the other countries finishing the job the Russians weren't able to do.*

*There was a general mobilizing of the Israeli army then, now swelled up to include the new immi-grants of the many nations that had originally fled to the holy land. No real war ensued back then, but the army was ready, just in case. News of mobilizations elsewhere around the globe also became more evi-dent every day. TV commentators began to speak of "total war" despite the general direction of peace that the world had taken earlier under the Leader's government.*

*That's when he had decided to take his family to Petra, where things were quiet. He had begun listen-ing to the rather detested One Hundred and Forty-Four Thousand, that group of maligned reactionary preachers who stood on soap boxes in the parks now and then and shouted about repentance and such tripe. They seemed at first a throwback to the unhappy times of Christianity, that narrow-minded discipline that had disappeared, thankfully, before the Leader's government had been formed. But these preachers had somehow begun to make sense to him even before their predictions starting coming true.*

*The evangelists had warned about the Leader and the Temple, and everyone thought at the time that it was just so much political trash. They were often jailed to quiet their clamoring, and few people had cared when their followers were occasionally ex-ecuted publicly as a warning. After all, every gov-*

*ernment has its dissenters, and they couldn't be allowed to get out of hand.*

*But they had been right about some things and he had begun to listen to them. They had recommended Petra, and by that time he was ready for any solution to the dangerous situation going on in Israel and the world in general. Petra wasn't exciting, but it seemed safe.*

*But he had made a mistake. He had returned to Jerusalem. It was to be a quick trip—just a visit to an ailing friend in a hospital. But he had come at a very bad time. His friend was practically delirious and was raving about Armageddon, an illegal Biblical term that the Leader had forbidden in political discussion. "Go to the One Hundred and Forty-Four Thousand," his friend had shouted, in his drugged state. "It's almost too late. They'll help you. It's your only chance!"*

*There was something compelling about the dangerous advice, and he had decided to seek out one of those hush-hush basement meetings of the revolutionary group. He had stopped on the way out of the hospital to ask a street beggar, undoubtedly one of the evangelists, where he might attend a meeting. The beggar, crippled and blind, whispered an address in the Old City and said, "Blessed is He who comes in the name of the Lord," a slogan of the dissenters.*

*But he had almost never gotten to the meeting. Jerusalem had all but blown up in his face that day! There had been sudden bombings, fires everywhere, soldiers in the streets. He had nearly panicked, but he made his way, doorway to doorway, to the address the beggar had given him. He may have blacked out for a time—he couldn't understand what was happening, but it was as if Jerusalem had suddenly been hit from all sides by marauding soldiers. He knew only that he had to get to that address and ask them what it all meant.*

*He had finally made it, and they had told him simply that Armageddon was virtually on them. Israel was to be torn to pieces by huge armies of virtually every nation. There had been no warning because the news of the impending crisis had been skillfully suppressed by the Leader's media workers, but the Bible had revealed it all anyway. The group had a Bible in the meeting, the only one he'd seen in the nearly seven years since he'd come to Israel from the U.S. He well knew that reading the ancient Scriptures carried the death penalty, and he resolved that if he survived this new holocaust he would never tell on them.*

*There had been a lot of people assembled in that darkened room, and a speaker in a wheelchair addressed them with the most remarkable ideas he had ever heard. It was the end of the world, the evangelist said. They had only one chance to survive, and that was to make their way to the Mount of Olives, where they would find, of all people, Jesus Christ!*

*It was impossible to believe—the ravings of a madman—but somehow, in the imminent fear of death, and the knowledge in his heart that there was no other way, he had forced himself to listen. Jesus was the Messiah all along, the speaker said, and the events now befalling Israel were clearly predicted in the Scriptures. The speaker quoted appropriate passages from the Bible, and in an uncanny way, the Biblical passages perfectly matched the story of the past seven years. He was mystified and, as the dissenters put it, "convicted."*

*Outside, the sound of explosions and airplanes— the horrors of full-scale war—increased as they listened. It all began to form a picture in his mind.*

*"Our hour has come," the speaker concluded. "Blessed is He who comes in the name of the Lord." They shouted as a body, repeating the mysterious formula, and he shouted with them, knowing as he uttered the Biblical phrase that he truly believed it.*

*And now he was in the Kidron Valley, moving slowly, terrified, from tree to tree and rock to rock. There were machine-gun bullets hitting all around him. Heavy shells hit the hills in front. The Temple, only half a mile behind his present position, was a wall of flames that lit the night. Horrible explosions racked the city of Jerusalem.*

*"I'm coming, Lord," was all he could think of.*

*Suddenly there was a tremendous wrenching roar from the Mount of Olives ahead of him. The world seemed to crunch in two at that impossible crashing sound. His ears went dead and his head was wracked through with terrible pain.*

*But his eyes were working and he looked up, half in terror, half in hope.*

*And there before him, in majesty and splendor, stood, of all people . . . Jesus Christ!*

Woe to the inhabiters of the earth and of the sea! For the devil is come down unto you, having great wrath, because he knoweth that he hath but a short time. And when the dragon saw that he was cast unto the earth, he persecuted the woman which brought forth the manchild.

—Revelation 12:12,13

Israel's troubles will only have begun at the time of the Rapture. Notwithstanding her longsuffering past, the worst is yet to come.

In that foreboding message from Revelation, the dragon represents Satan, who never tires of Jewish blood. The woman pictures Israel and the manchild is, of course, Israel's most noted offspring, Jesus Christ. One can understand the Devil's aversion to the Messiah and His homeland, for together they will prove his undoing.

The Devil has done his dirty work on Israel all along, as we have seen; tyrants invariably detest the irrepressible Jews. But the time of the Rapture, the church's hour of triumph, is ironically the start of Israel's greatest agony. When the trumpet sounds and the church goes home, the Jews will begin to endure a fate worse than any that befell them during the entire 4000-year tragedy that has been their experience on this earth.

We have noted that the trumpet signals the Jews to go home to their promised land (Isaiah 27:13), and we have suggested that this homegoing will be under duress. The seven-year period of Tribulation which follows the Rapture will introduce suffering in Israel such as even that longsuffering land has never seen before. Jeremiah labeled it "the time of Jacob's trouble" (Jeremiah 30:7), and the Messiah Himself coined the term "the Great Tribulation" (Matthew 24:21).

It will be a time of awesome judgment upon the world, and Israel will be purged and purified by God Himself.

Zechariah's detailed scenarios of the end times inform us of a terrifying casualty rate in Tribulation-period Israel:

> And it shall come to pass, that in all the land, saith the Lord, two parts therein shall be cut off and die; but the third shall be left therein.
>
> —Zechariah 13:8

Two-thirds of Israel is to perish! To give this a number, there are now about 14 million Jews in the world. Should the Tribulation period come upon us very soon, something like nine million Jews will die. Even Hitler's maniacal extermination program did not account for this many Jewish deaths; six million were lost in the Nazi slaughter.

But only five million Jews will survive the horrors of the Tribulation and survive until the second coming of the Lord.

What is God's purpose in all this? Has He decided at last to turn His back on His chosen people?

Actually, Zechariah makes clear that God intends for the remaining third of the people to experience the greatest of spiritual blessings:

> And I will bring the third part through the fire, and will refine them as silver is refined, and will try them as gold is tried; they shall call on my name, and I will hear them: I will say, It is my people, and they shall say, The Lord is my God.
>
> —Zechariah 13:9

At the very end, as we have seen, "All Israel shall be saved" (Romans 11:26), and at least these surviving millions will greet their King. It has never been more than a remnant of the Jewish people who have accepted their Messiah in any generation since the time of Christ, but this remnant has always received His blessings, as they will at the end.

Israel will thus become the world's first Christian nation, after God's trial by fire, and the Messiah will at last be recognized and honored by His people.

It's a tough way to come home, but it is apparently necessary because of Israel's long-standing aversion to her Messiah. The official Jewish policy has always been that Jesus was not the Messiah—that at best He was a misunderstood Rabbi and at worst a deceiving blasphemer—and thus any Jews who have believed in Him have been regarded as traitors. So God's purification of His people is apparently unavoidable.

We could just as well say, of course, that God will be coming down on the Gentiles too, because they will also suffer a great reduction of their numbers in the Tribulation period. No Gentile nation has ever come to Christ as a body either; only a small minority of Gentiles are true believers in the Messiah. The Jewish community normally estimates that 1 percent of their number are Christian believers; one wonders if 1 percent of the world's Gentiles are Christian believers!

The Jews today, like the majority of the Gentiles, are not really believers in anything Biblical. The highly orthodox Jews carry out varying amounts of traditional Law, roughly based on the Scriptures but more usually on the rabbinical commentaries of bygone days. The chosen people are more likely to embrace modern-day agnosticism, with each new generation blending more completely with our present-day pagan world.

Obviously, it will take radical spiritual surgery to reconcile this very special people, God's chosen ones, to their Creator. Strong illness requires strong medicine.

It will not be the first time that God has dealt this way with the Jews. In fact, the procedure of purification by duress has been repeated throughout their history. When the early Jews rejected the promised land in favor of fertile Egypt, slavery resulted for the nation. When the nation was divided into two kingdoms following the reigns of David and Solomon and became idolatrous, they were conquered and detained in Babylon for 70 years; the land and the Temple were left a shambles. Finally, when the Messiah came and went largely unrecognized by His own people, the second Temple was destroyed and the nation was dispersed throughout the world.

In each case the Jews were able to pull themselves back together dramatically, against heavy odds, and restore themselves. The most recent recovery is the founding of Israel by the modern Jews, an event totally unforeseen except by their prophets.

So history will repeat itself. There will be a decimation of the nation again, on a scale never suffered before, and then reconciliation to God on a spiritual level never before achieved by any nation. So goes the saga of Israel, God's own people.

Concerning Satan's interest in the Jews (as revealed both in Revelation and by world history), the Devil is a student of Scripture. He realizes that his own final doom is linked inevitably with Israel and the return of Christ to the earth. He apparently reasons that if he can destroy Israel, the Messianic plans of God might fall apart. Jesus would have no nation to come home to; there would be no Jews crying, "Blessed is He who comes in the name of the Lord." The whole idea of an ultimately triumphant chosen people would have been thwarted, and a key part of God's plan would have been ruined.

Satan's strategy is clear—the prophets have seen it all. He will use both the totally obedient Antichrist and the pagan hordes of the world to once more abuse the Jews.

It will begin innocently enough; the Devil has always been a diplomat. The Antichrist will step forward with apparent help for Israel and the world. He will appear to be an angel of light, with loads of ideas about how to solve the world's problems. To Israel he will offer something for which they would trade almost anything—security. He will make a seven-year agreement with the Jews (Daniel 9:27a), apparently to protect their borders, and they will seem to be satisfied with the treaty, at least at the beginning.

We picture this treaty as following the coming Russian invasion of Israel, which we place at the beginning of the Tribulation period.* The Antichrist will say, in effect, "You were lucky this time; you need protection; I really admire you Jews," etc., etc.

They'll buy his line—at least until the moment when he shows his true colors.

At the middle of the Tribulation period the Antichrist will renege on his part of the agreement, enter the Temple of Jerusalem (which will then be in use for normal Jewish worship), and proclaim himself God!** Daniel warns, "In the midst of the week he shall cause the sacrifice and the oblation to cease . . ." (Daniel 9:27), and Paul spells out the details: ". . . he, as God, sitteth in the temple of God, showing himself that he is God" (2 Thessalonians 2:4).

This one-of-a-kind blasphemy will trigger the horrible second half of the seven-year period, known as the Great Tribulation. The Antichrist is at least as stiff-necked as the chosen people, and when they oppose his tactless arrogance he will virtually call the

*See *The Coming Russian Invasion of Israel,* by McCall and Levitt, Moody Press, 1974.
**See *Satan in the Sanctuary,* by McCall and Levitt, Moody Press, 1973.

world to war. The Jews are rebels, he will say, finding an excuse like so many tyrants before him to annihilate the chosen people.

Jesus gave a word to the wise about these hard times to come:

> Then let them which be in Judea flee into the mountains. Let him which is on the housetop not come down to take anything out of his house, neither let him which is in the field return back to take his clothes. And woe unto them that are with child, and to them that give suck in those days! But pray ye that your flight be not in winter, neither on the sabbath day, for then shall be great tribulation, such as was not since the beginning of the world to this time, no, nor ever shall be.
> —Matthew 24:16-21

The Jews are to get out, fast, without stopping to pack any belongings. The Lord went on sadly, "And except those days should be shortened, there should be no flesh be saved . . ." (Matthew 24:22).

In the last holocaust, in Germany, too many Jews lingered to take care of their belongings as the Nazis organized their diabolical slaughter. No one wants to run for it, to leave his home and possessions, just because of a dictatorial government. It is more natural to try to stick it out.

But this time, in the Tribulation period, if a Jew is on his roof fixing his TV antenna, he is to jump to the ground and keep on going, as the Lord pictures it. Little comfort is offered to pregnant women or mothers of infants. The details of the prophecy supply the totality of the devastation.

The Antichrist will supervise the most spectacular world war ever suffered by the race of man following his falling-out with Israel. It will apparently take the rest of the Tribulation period, some 3½ years, just to get it all together! A 200-million-man army will march from the East (usually thought to be China), the ten-nation confederacy of Europe will join the fray, and on and on it will go. Everybody will be invited!

The details of Armageddon are clear to most Bible readers, and the possibilities of global war are all too clear to thinking people everywhere today. Suffice it to say, as the Lord put it, that if He didn't call an early end to this conflict all life on earth would perish.

The Apostle John saw this ultimate war as the final supernatural battle between God and Satan. God will pour out His wrath on the world throughout the Tribulation period and Satan will attempt to drown Israel in total war. That is the physical picture of things to come.

Spiritually, something else will be going on behind the scenes. The Tribulation period can obviously be seen as seven years of utter devastation for Israel, but it is also seven years of progressive sanctifying. Through the events of this hard sojourn, Israel will gradually come to realize the validity and ultimately the physical presence of Jesus, her promised Messiah.

At the very beginning of the Tribulation, the Jews will come home to their land, in fulfillment of many Old Testament prophecies. True, it will be under the duress of persecution that the Jews will gather themselves in Israel, but the great homecoming theme, already recognized in this time of Israel's reestablishment, will suggest to devout Jews the beginning of the end.

Then the Russian invasion will come, but the enemy will be vanquished. This surprising annihilation of vastly superior forces will serve to demonstrate to Israel that God is very much alive and well, and is still fulfilling His promises to them. It won't require a seminary graduate to understand in Ezekiel's prophecy God's rationale for delivering His people on this occasion:

> So the house of Israel shall know that I am the Lord their God from that day and forward.
> —Ezekiel 39:22

All the while the 144,000 Hebrew Christian evangelists will be spelling out just what is happening from a spiritual point of view (Revelation 7:3-8). They may not draw very big crowds, but as events progress through the seven years their message will become more and more meaningful.

When the Antichrist enters the Temple for his blasphemy, Israel will really sit up and take notice. That this is a spiritual matter should be clear to even the most marginal of Jewish worshipers, and of course the 144,000 will certainly bring out the Scriptures to explain what is happening. More than a few salvations should result as the Jews consider the correlation between the Biblically recorded events and the current goings-on in their land.

It will be much easier to explain prophecy in those coming times!

The extreme peril of Armageddon will be the final proof that God's plan is progressing as announced, and the appearance of the King Himself will set off the mammoth national redemption in Israel. At last the entire nation will cry with Isaiah, "All we like sheep have gone astray . . . and the Lord has laid on Him the iniquity of us all" (Isaiah 53:6), and the surviving Jews will at last utter their special password to the Kingdom, "Blessed is He who comes in the name of the Lord."

What an altar call! At least five million saved!

So the Jews will finally "look upon Him whom they have pierced" (Zechariah 12:10), and they will believe and be saved. As for Armageddon, the Lord and His mighty host, the returning church, will sweep it away. Revelation gives no picture of a lengthy battle as the Lord returns to end "the war to end all wars."

The agony of Israel will then be over for all time. The trumpet will have sounded just seven years earlier, and it will have been a long seven years, but through the time of Jacob's trouble the chosen people will at last have found God permanently. They will join with the church at that triumphant time to form the kingdom of Christ on the earth, the thousand-year reign called the Millennium.

# Chapter 6

# THE KING
# IS COMING!

*Heaven was, and always had been . . . "heavenly."
He had certainly enjoyed his last few centuries!*

*Ever since he had come to heaven, at the time of
the Spanish Inquisition, he had been truly happy.
The presence of the Lord and of the believers of
past times, coupled with the knowledge that the
kingdom on earth was ever nearer, all contributed to
his unending happiness. The concepts of heaven that
men held during his past earthly life had been somewhat inaccurate in detail, but the idea of true happiness—continuous joy—was certainly correct. Life
had never been like this on earth!*

*But even better times were yet to come! Soon the
Rapture would take place, and millions more saints
would join them for the great marriage of the Lamb
in heaven. Then they would all go back to the earth*

with the Lord for His glorious thousand-year reign, the Millennium. And then eternity! He would really need all of eternity to appreciate all this happiness!

The Rapture was an event as eagerly awaited among the saints in heaven as among those still on the earth. He and his brothers in heaven longed for that great moment when they would be united with their former bodies and then changed. Life in his earthly body had been good and bad; life now, in his spiritual existence, was glorious. But the life to come, in his immortal resurrection body—that's what he longed for! His new incorruptible flesh awaited only the moment of the Rapture, and he longed for it like the other millions of saints in heaven.

The anticipation had grown almost unbearable in its joy with the recent developments. The Jews had come back to Israel, and he had thought that the wild cheering of the saints above would be heard on the earth! And then they had recovered Jerusalem, the future capital city of the Lord's earthly government. All was in readiness for that great moment when the Lord would lead them to the clouds to gather up their brothers and sisters in Christ.

The saints had begun singing a new hymn then, "The King is Going." They could almost hear the trumpet sounding!

He longed for those great moments to come. He would receive his martyr's crown, and he longed to present it to the King when the earthly saints had all come marching in. He exulted in his martyrdom now, but he remembered how fearful he had been about it during his earthly life.

It had been sad. The misguided unbelievers, filled with hatred and bigotry, had pursued the true believers and the Jews so cruelly. So many had died such terrible deaths in those Inquisitions. He had known when they arrested him what he would do; he would trust the Lord. He would pray and he would remain faithful, and when they would demand that he renounce his faith, he would stand fast. He would follow the example of the Lord at His own trial, going as a lamb to the slaughter.

How it grieved the Father, he now knew, to see the chosen people and the church of God tortured and murdered by the pagans. How the Holy Spirit had labored to strengthen them in those hard times.

He had held to his love of the Lord even though the inquisitors had beaten and burned him, and he had longed for what his torturers thought of as death, but what he knew in his heart was truly life. He had cried for the Jews, indomitable and uncompromising as always, and he had cried for the Father as the Jews were killed.

When he himself was tied to the stake he had tried to calm his own mind and force his thoughts to his inquisitors. At the very end he had done well, serving his Lord—he had managed to pray for his torturers.

That was hard. He was in terrible pain at the end. But he had said what he knew was just and holy to say, "Forgive them, Father." He had cried out to the Father then, and suddenly the pain was ended.

It was still a difficult memory, and he now knew how the saints in heaven had been affected by those times, and by so many other terrible earthly times. Abraham had watched so much horror in his long time in heaven. The apostles of the Lord had grieved so often through the centuries.

He had been instantly in heaven then, out of his

poor, abused flesh, and he had remained in his spiritual existence ever since. His flesh had been hard to manage in life, and hard in death, but he now looked forward to being with it again, to be changed.

There had been happy times through the centuries in heaven as the saints watched the progress of the church on earth. Everything wasn't torture and death in man's existence, and he had exulted with the multitudes at each small, simple godly act down through the centuries. Each time a soul was saved the community of heaven had grown by one, and many were saved by the faithful. The Holy Spirit was active in the world and the Lord was engaged in intercession for the believers. But the Devil was active too, and they often waited in suspense over the contest of wills.

It was a great joy to greet the new souls as they constantly arrived, and it was an immense pleasure to see the new arrivals realize the magnificence of God's fulfilled promise. But the big event was imminent, they all knew, and it was beginning to eclipse everything else. How they wanted to get to the Rapture! How he longed to encounter again his broken, burned flesh, which the Lord would so marvelously restore! Only God could undo such horrible work on the part of Satan, and he was ever thankful to be with God!

And then everything was ready on earth at last! The last soul had been saved in the church, and events had prepared God's judgment, the dread Tribulation. The Antichrist was ready to perform his deadly work, and the moment had come to rescue and reward the believers. They couldn't wait any longer!

They massed in a huge multitude behind the Lord

*Himself. How magnificent He was, about to accomplish this huge harvest of saved souls. All heaven shown with the glory of God.*

*At a signal from the Lord, the trumpet was raised.*

An old Jewish proverb says that where there are two Jews there are three opinions.

Quibbling is a big part of the *other* chosen people, too—Christians have founded 263 American church denominations, not to mention those of the rest of the world, and it seems that no two saints can fully agree on anything! The 263 denominations aren't necessarily at war, of course; often the disagreement is so slight as to escape the members of the congregations themselves.

But where the Rapture is concerned, it's almost theological war.

Some people think the Rapture comes *before* the Tribulation period, as the authors do. Others think it comes *in the middle of* that seven-year period. And still others think it comes *at the end of* that period. And some think it isn't coming at all!

# THE KING IS COMING!

For convenience in arguing, the various positions go by short names in theological circles—pre-trib (ulation), mid-trib, post-trib, and a-trib, respectively. It seems that some of the most eminent scholars hold differing views among these positions, and that each school of thought can support its view with at least a certain amount of Scriptural evidence.

But all these positions can't be right; they are all mutually exclusive. And the issue is quite important, to say the least. Christians certainly must have varying outlooks on life according to whether they think they are to escape the coming Tribulation or endure it here on earth!

This controversy was given a very complete airing in the May 1974 issue of *Christian Life* magazine, which was a special issue devoted to the topic "Jesus is Coming Again." A relevant leading article by Hal Lindsey (pre-trib) gave his (and the Biblical prophets') "Predictions of Things To Come," and then four well-known scholars held forth on the four-way controversy about the time and reality of the Rapture.

The senior author of this book was the representative in this particular forum for the pre-trib point of view. Dr. McCall held that Christ's return for the Rapture is imminent (which means He may claim His church at any moment) and that the Tribulation period will follow the Rapture, just as we have explained throughout this book.

We are convinced that the pre-tribulation scenario of the Rapture that we have given is the correct one, but we also feel that a fair discussion of all positions, along with our critiques, would be a good policy in any book about the Rapture. Thus we are going to give the reasons for our view in this chapter, and the various other positions, along with their evidence, in the next chapter.

But make no mistake about it: we think the King is coming and *soon!*

The simplest piece of evidence for a pre-trib Rapture lies in the announcement that Jesus will come for His own "like a thief in the night." His appearance at the Rapture will come as a complete surprise; He will, in effect, sneak up on us like a burglar. He warns us to be ready at all times, since we cannot know the exact moment.

This concept is shattered by a mid-trib or post-trib Rapture simply because it would be quite easy for us to calculate the Lord's arrival from what we know about prophecy. With either of those views we would need only to note the time when the Tribulation begins (when the Antichrist makes his peace convenant with Israel) and then count off the days until the midpoint (1260 days, as given in Revelation 11:3) or the ending point (seven years after the beginning, as given in Daniel 9:27—his seventieth "week" of seven years each).

We could virtually be packed and ready to go when the Lord came, and He could hardly approach like a "thief in the night" under those circumstances.

And this situation brings up the whole bugaboo of people making ready at the last moment for the Kingdom. Why live the Christian life, with all its difficulties and self-discipline, someone could well ask, when we can just arrange to receive Christ shortly before the Rapture and go to be with Him anyway?

Instead, the surprise approach of the Lord demands that we remain in spiritual readiness and promotes the pursuit of a suitable testimony. We musn't be caught napping, as it were.

Secondly, the Rapture belongs to the church, as its reward, while the Tribulation period belongs to the world as its just retribution. The Tribulation period is equivalent to Daniel's seventieth week, most Bible scholars agree, and Daniel's weeks concern the people of Israel, not the church. The Lord's angel, who gave Daniel this magnificent prophecy, specified that the "seventy weeks are determined upon *thy* people [Israel] and upon *thy* holy city [Jerusalem]" (Daniel 9:24). Israel, as we have seen, is distinct from the church (though saved Jews are part of the church, of course, and go up during the Rapture).

Thirdly, we can see from the Scripture that the Holy Spirit will be taken out of the world before the Antichrist is revealed. Paul informed the church at Thessalonica that "He who now letteth [restrains or hinders] will let until he be taken out of the way. And then shall that Wicked [one] be revealed" (2 Thessalonians 2:7,8). In other words, the Holy Spirit has inhibited the appearance of the Antichrist; when the Spirit goes, the Antichrist comes.

It follows that the church will be removed as the Spirit is removed, since the Holy Spirit's home on earth is the church, which He indwells. Thus we believers will leave before the appearance of the Antichrist, and so the Rapture will come before the Tribulation.

Paul continues in 2 Thessalonians by contrasting the mission of the Antichrist with the reward of the church; the Antichrist appears "that they [the world] might all be judged. . . . But God hath from the beginning chosen you to salvation" (see 2 Thessalonians 2:9-13).

Paul concludes this agreeable revelation with the heartening recommendation, "Therefore, brethren, stand fast, and hold the traditions which ye have been taught, whether by word or our epistle" (2 Thessalonians 2:15).

We might refer back to the logic of the Jewish feasts and their chronological formula on this point. The Spirit came, we saw, at the time of Pentecost, observed in late springtime. This feast began the period of the harvest, and of course the Holy Spirit is the great Harvester in the world. The Spirit began His ministry at Pentecost with a harvest of 3000 souls at that dramatic Temple-site scene in which the simple Galileans found themselves the masters of some 16 foreign tongues. The Spirit's ministry goes on today in the church age, since we have not yet finished the harvest. We have not yet heard the trumpet, and so we continue to harvest with the Spirit's help.

But at the sound of the trumpet the harvest is over, as we have seen. There are no crops to harvest after autumn, of course; the fields have already produced their yield for the year. The Day of Atonement comes next, with its final rulings on judgment and redemption.

This symbol seems to demonstrate that the age of the church—the very work of the church—is completed at the time of the Rapture. What is left are the rewards and results of what has gone before—redemption for the church and judgment for the world.

Our symbology would fail if the church were to remain on earth during the Tribulation period, awaiting a later Rapture. In view of Paul's instructions to the Thessalonians, we would have two mutually exclusive processes going on at once—the church would be witnessing and harvesting, and the Antichrist would be punishing them. Also, we get the feeling from Scripture that the Antichrist has little trouble setting up his kingdom in the Tribulation period; he is readily accepted. This would be very hard to picture if the church were present in the world; many millions of people would be objecting, publishing books, warning the masses, and so forth.

The Antichrist's relatively easy takeover is explained very simply if we realize that the church has already been raptured away. Then the unbelievers, left to their own devices, will easily fall prey to a false religion.

A final, very big reason why the Rapture comes before the Tribulation period is that the Rapture requires no signs or events to happen before it. It was regarded as an imminent possibility back in the first-century church! Titus 2:13 reminds us to be constantly "looking for that blessed hope, and the glorious appearing of the great God and our Saviour, Jesus Christ." Paul felt that single people might well not worry about marriage because the imminent return of the Lord was possible, and that would certainly change everyone's status anyway. (I Corinthians 7:29).

Surely there would be no point in remaining in readiness for an event which has to be preceded by observable events which haven't happened yet! But the mid-trib and post-trib positions assert that Tribulation-period events *must* happen before the Rapture.

The Tribulation period is filled with signs and

warnings. The Antichrist makes his covenant with Israel, a world government is formed, the Antichrist desecrates the Temple, and Armageddon occurs, to mention just a few events. If the church were present on earth during all of these events, the Scriptural admonitions for us to await an imminent return of the Lord would be meaningless. We would only have to watch the newspapers. And the Apostle would have been giving poor advice when he told the church to wait for the Lord so long ago.

Because no events have to precede the Rapture, we expect it at any moment.

This thinking ought to make a big difference to all of us. We certainly ought to rejoice that the Lord means to spare us punishment; we only regret that more of the world does not come to the saving power of Christ and avoid the coming consequences of the Tribulation period. That will be a most tragic and difficult time for everyone on the earth, as we have seen. In our Savior's words, "For then shall be great tribulation, such as was not since the beginning of the world to this time, no, nor ever shall be" (Matthew 24:21).

In a sense, we would *expect* to be delivered from this punishment—we who believe. God has acted this way before. Lot and his family were spared at Sodom when a wrathful God gave sinners their just deserts. Noah and his sons and their wives were spared the calamity of the Flood by carrying out the explicit instructions of God, just as they always had.

When Elijah cried out in frustration over the chosen people's irreverence, even wanting God to slay them all, the patient God of creation pointed out that there were still 7000 people who had not bowed the knee to Baal. It was a paltry number, but they were precious to God and they were spared.

The theme of the gospel of Jesus Christ is forgiveness, at least to those who believe. The sacrifice of our Lord accomplished the exoneration of sinners who would recognize Him and His gift of salvation.

We could only expect to be spared the judgment of the world that will come from a just God.

But we have said that others hold other views, and that they are believers, too. The Bible is a cryptic and complex book, requiring much study and application. Some of its concepts have never been explained to date, while others promote differences even among knowledgeable commentators.

We give you now, in a spirit of fairness, some of those other views.

## Chapter 7

# PRE-TRIB? MID-TRIB? POST-TRIB? A-TRIB?

*Pilgrim felt light as a cloud—free and unfettered. His heavy load had been taken off his back, and it was a tremendous relief. He had known it was burdensome, but just how heavy it was he had never known until at last it slid from his shoulders.*

*It had been a long journey, but he had finally come to Christ the Lord, and now he stood a forgiven man. He was a new creature—reborn and aware that a new journey had just begun. Yet there were certain obstacles and pitfalls along the way of eternal life.*

*Not long afterward, Pilgrim found himself in the Tunnel of Prophecy. It was dark and tortuous, full of mysterious twists and turns. Pilgrim had difficulty finding his way and keeping from stumbling into dead-end side paths.*

*Suddenly Pilgrim was confronted by the Monster, Post-Trib!*

*Pilgrim stood his ground hesitantly as Post-Trib glared down at him. "Get ready to endure," intoned Post-Trib menacingly. "The Great Tribulation comes!" Post-Trib went on to warn Pilgrim that the church was soon to face the most difficult days of its whole existence, and that Pilgrim, along with the other believers, was to watch for the rise of the Antichrist, the abomination of desolation, and the War of Armageddon.*

*There was no time to waste, Post-Trib said. Survival training for the coming Tribulation was imperative at once. It wasn't a very happy message, all in all.*

*Pilgrim replied, in all politeness, that he thought he was supposed to watch for the Lord, not the Antichrist, and that he understood that Jesus could come at any moment. But Post-Trib said in reply that Jesus had stated that He would return at the end of the Tribulation period. Pilgrim had better understand that the worst was yet to come. As he departed he cried out, "Get ready for the Tribulation!"*

*It hadn't been a very happy interview for Pilgrim, who continued wearily through the dark tunnel. There seemed to be very little light in the Tunnel of Prophecy.*

*Soon there came along a very short fellow, a midget, named Mid-Trib. He stared up at Pilgrim, seeing how sorrowful he was, and inquired what the matter was. Pilgrim revealed the message of Post-Trib—the glum news about the believers going through the Tribulation.*

*"Oh, I wouldn't belief the half of it," said Mid-Trib. "The last half of it, that is."*

*"What are you trying to tell me?" asked Pilgrim, hoping for some good news at last.*

*The diminutive believer smiled and said, "Don't be so worried about the Tribulation. You don't have to go through the whole thing—just half of it. You just have to watch for that blasphemy by the Antichrist, right in the middle of the whole affair, and then . . . away you go!"*

*Pilgrim was a bit perplexed. The view of Mid-Trib was twice as comforting as that of Post-Trib, one might think, but it still seemed rather melancholy that the believers would have to endure the first half of the coming Tribulation. "I thought those seven years, Daniel's seventieth week, was between the Antichrist and Israel. What does the church have to do with it?"*

*But the midget brought him up short. "Just watch for that 'abomination of desolation'—that's the sign of the Rapture!" he shouted, and he disappeared down the tunnel.*

*No sooner had the echo of Mid-Trib's warning faded than Pilgrim caught sight of the two brothers, Past-Trib and A-Trib. They weren't twins, Pilgrim saw, but they looked a lot alike. They seemed in quite good spirits, and Pilgrim soon learned that they were celebrating the fact that there was to be no Tribulation period at all! The church wouldn't have to go through it, and neither would anyone else, because there was simply no such thing, they exulted.*

*Before Pilgrim could ask any questions, however, they began to argue between themselves. A-Trib said the whole idea of a Tribulation period was just a tall story, and Past-Trib took offense, saying that there* had indeed been a Tribulation period long ago, just after Christ's first coming.

The two quelled their bickering long enough to assure Pilgrim that the Lord's second coming was imminent and that Christ would then complete everything. There was nothing special to watch for, and especially "No Tribulation for you to be concerned about."

Pilgrim was very thoughtful about what they had said as they trailed off, lost in debating their differences. Their messages just didn't seem to match up with the Lord's own words about the "last days," as well as the frightening visions of the Revelation. Why would such end-time passages be included in God's Word if they weren't to be heeded? He didn't feel he could accept their views, nor break into their argument for discussion.

The Tunnel of Prophecy seemed to be brightening as Pilgrim went along, and he thought he could see some light in the dim distance. He rounded a bend, though, and almost stumbled into the foreboding, military figure of Marshal Partial.

The Marshal's stern visage shone with offended righteousness as he warned Pilgrim that the Rapture was not for everyone. "Just because you're a Christian doesn't mean you will be taken in the Rapture," admonished the Marshal. "You have to be absolutely ready for the Lord when he comes!" He touched the tips of his mustache and concluded, "Otherwise you will have to go through the Tribulation with the rest of the world!"

As Pilgrim talked further with Marshal Partial he found him unsure of the salvation of most Christians—himself included! "You doubt your own salvation?" asked Pilgrim, very troubled for the man.

*Pilgrim's own mind was quite settled on this important point. He just did not doubt the Lord's promise of eternal life for the believer, and he believed the Scriptures where they said "We shall all" be changed at the Rapture, not "some."*

*Marshal Partial seemed deep in thought, having worried himself into a frowning countenance, but Pilgrim did not want to pause with him any longer. The tunnel seemed to be getting lighter and lighter, and he wanted to find the end of it more than ever. So he strode away in the direction of the light.*

*As Pilgrim moved into the light the truth dawned on him in a new way. There* would *be a Rapture for all believers; it was imminent; it would come before the terrible Tribulation. Pilgrim and the church had only to await the Lord's pleasure as to the time, but they would go to be with Him forever!*

*As he at last broke forth from the tunnel he saw a pleasant-looking man awaiting him. Pre-Trib greeted him kindly and walked with him from then on along His expectant journey.*

We should stress, to begin with, that we don't know when the King is coming.

If you bought this book to find out the date of the Rapture, you bought the wrong book. Taking a choice among the various positions about the time of the Rapture will inform you a great deal about what to watch for (or not bother watching for!) but it won't give you the day, month, and year of Christ's coming. That's not available, according to the Lord.

*But as we said, it's only fair to spell out the major*

*choices available, along with our commentary on each one.*

# THE VARIOUS POSITIONS

An outline of the various positions concerning the time of the Rapture was given by Dr. McCall in the *Christian Life* article we cited in the preceding chapter. These are the definitions.

## PRE-TRIBULATION RAPTURE

All true believers in Christ will be caught up in the air to go with the Lord to heaven suddenly, at any moment, before the Tribulation begins. The Rapture will include all believers throughout the church age, whether living or dead, at which time they will receive their eternal heavenly bodies, like Christ's resurrection body. Following the Rapture is the Tribulation, the return of Christ to the earth, the Millennium, and the eternal new heaven and new earth.

## POST-TRIBULATION RAPTURE

Believers will continue on the earth through the Tribulation period. At the end of the Tribulation, believers will be caught up to be with the Lord and immediately return to earth with Him for the Millennium.

## MID-TRIBULATION RAPTURE

Believers will remain on the earth for the first 3½ years of the 7-year Tribulation and will be caught up before the last 3½ years (the "Great Tribulation") falls upon the human race.

## PARTIAL RAPTURE

Only spiritual believers in Christ will be caught up before the Tribulation. Carnal believers will have to suffer through the wrath of the Tribulation along with the rest of the world.

## PAST-TRIBULATION RAPTURE

The Tribulation has already occurred in past history, and therefore it will not reoccur in the future. Christ will return to Rapture the church and immediately take the church back to earth for the Millennium.

## NO RAPTURE

There is no Rapture, no Tribulation period, no Millennium. Believers look forward only to the eternal state of heaven in the future.

That's a lot of theories about one event (or non-event)! We'll discuss them in sequence, giving as best we can the Scriptural basis of each position plus our own evaluation.

It should be borne in mind that we uncompromisingly hold to the pretribulation Rapture position as given first above. Conceivably more eloquent spokesmen could be found for the others, but in the spirit of covering the subject as adequately and evenhandedly as possible in this space, we offer the following discussion. Perhaps a more complete understanding of the views will serve to promote harmony among the protagonists.

For the moment we will omit a discussion of the

pretribulation position as it is given through this book.

## POST-TRIB RAPTURE

The post-trib thinker emphasizes the idea that the Scriptures never seem to clearly distinguish between the Rapture and the second coming. He assumes the two to be one event, or to occur simultaneously. This position is referred to as the "unity of the second coming."

True enough, Jesus' messages about the future in His dramatic last days on earth made no distinction between the two heartening promises. He told His disciples that they would suffer tribulation but that they would be delivered by His return (Matthew 23:29-31). He also told them that He would come back and "receive you unto myself" (John 14:1-3) in the future Rapture. Because He did not refer to any time period between the two events, the post-trib advocate holds that they are simultaneous—virtually the same event. Christ will Rapture the church and return with the church to end the Tribulation in one action, according to this view.

Another argument for the unity of the second coming concerns our trumpet symbol. We noted Paul's specifications of the trumpet at the Rapture (1 Thessalonians 4:16; 1 Corinthians 15:52), the "last trump". The post-trib believer points out that the Lord also mentioned a trumpet sounding—but at the end of the Tribulation. That's accurate—the Lord definitely specified the trumpet in connection with His return to earth at His second coming (Matthew 24:29-31).

The logic here is that if Paul's trumpet is the

"last" trumpet, and if a trumpet sounds at the end of the Tribulation, they are the same trumpet. Paul's Rapture trumpet is the Lord's second-coming announcement trumpet, the reasoning goes, and so the Rapture comes at the end of the Tribulation.

Then there is the argument from 2 Thessalonians 2:1-5, that two unmistakable events must occur before the Rapture—the great apostasy and the blasphemy by the Antichrist. 2 Thessalonians 2:3 states clearly, "Let no man deceive you by any means: for that day shall not come except there come a falling away first, and that man of sin be revealed, the son of perdition."

Since these two events are clearly Tribulation-period events, the Tribulation must come before the Rapture.

Those arguments, probably the best of the Scriptural arguments for the post-trip position, seem very logical, and it is understandable that many people subscribe to them.

It may sound as though we're really stuck. However, a careful examination of these very Scriptures provides a different and, we think, still more logical view.

First of all, the unity of the second coming is not really a necessary conclusion from the fact that the Lord did not separate events by time. His mention of the Rapture and the second coming without specifying a time separation follows an Old Testament precedent for Biblical style. The prophets sometimes described the first and second advents of Christ— events separated by more than 1900 years—in the same sentence (for instance, Micah 5:2)! In one breath Daniel spoke both of the tyrant Antiochus (165 B.C.) and the antichrist (Daniel 8)! Why should the Lord have been expected to mention the passing of a mere seven years between the Rapture and the second coming?

As to the trumpet, the term "last" is an elastic term in Scripture. In the epistles the church age is referred to as the "last" age (Hebrews 1:2; 1 Peter 1:20; etc.), since the Messiah has come, but these last days have really gone on! When the "last trump" of the Rapture sounds it does not necessarily mean that no more trumpets can be blown, but merely that the last prophetic events have been set in motion.

Concerning the 2 Thessalonian 2 passage, which seems to say that the apostasy and the blasphemy must come before the Rapture: we think the Rapture is not being referred to here at all. The term used in 2 Thessalonians 2:2 is actually "the day of the Lord" (rather than "the day of Christ," as in the King James Version), and we think this phrase refers to Christ's second coming to earth rather than the Rapture.

As a matter of fact, this very passage may prove the pre-trib view. The "falling away" may not describe apostasy at all, but rather the removal of the church from the earth—a physical rather than spiritual "falling away." In this case the passage would say that the Rapture must come *before* the specified events.

If this sounds like nit-picking among Scriptures, it is, in a way, but the pre-trib view of the Rapture does not depend on delicate definitions of specific Scriptures. The main problem with the post-trib position has already been given—it violates the whole principle of the imminent reappearance of the Lord. We are told in hundreds of Scriptures—urged and entreated, in fact—to remain in constant readiness, "looking for the blessed hope" (Titus 2:13). We are warned that the Lord will come suddenly and unexpectedly, like lightning, "in the twinkling of an eye," "like a thief in the night," but in the post-trib view we could mark off days on a calendar for seven years before His appearance.

Furthermore, we wouldn't be in the position of looking for any "blessed hope"; in fact we would be looking for the gruesome signs of the Antichrist and his horrible Tribulation government. This hardly seems to be an appropriate reward for the believing church!

## MID-TRIB RAPTURE

The mid-trib Rapture folks stress the frequent mention in Scripture of that 3½-year midpoint of the Tribulation. They feel that the explanation of this constant theme is that this is the point when a big change occurs—the church is raptured at this point.

And true enough, the formula of 3½ years certainly is repeated many times by the prophets. It is variously given as "the midst" of the Tribulation, as "times, time, and half-a-time" ($2+1+\frac{1}{2}=3\frac{1}{2}$), as "42 months," and as "1260 days" (Hebrew year= 360 days. See Daniel 9:27 and Revelation 11:2).

The mid-trib Rapture involves the church remaining here on earth to be persecuted for the first 3½ years of the Tribulation, and Daniel 7:25 is usually cited to support this idea:

> And he shall speak great words against the Most High, and shall wear out the saints of the Most High, and think to change times and laws; and they shall be given into his hand until a time and times and the dividing of time [half a time].

Again, in Daniel 9:27, the prophet relates that "he [the Antichrist] shall confirm the covenant with many for one week, and in the midst of the week he shall cause the sacrifice and oblation to cease. . . ." The interpretation is often made that the "many" in this Scripture refers to the church, and that it is they who make a seven-year agreement with the Antichrist. Their worship ("the sacrifice and the oblation") ceases at the midpoint of the agreement because the Rapture then occurs.

We find these arguments a little hazy in view of more sound readings of these same Scriptures. To begin with, the 3½-year point in the Tribulation certainly *is* significant, but it is nowhere connected to the Rapture. Its significance lies in the Antichrist's blasphemy and in Israel's resulting recoil, which ultimately leads to Armageddon. It is as if the Antichrist at this point shows his true colors, after 3½ years of relative peace under his regime. When he enters the Tribulation Temple to show the world that he is God, the Antichrist in effect shows Israel and the believers present on earth that he is really more like Satan. The very idea of the Devil represented directly in the Temple of God—"Satan in the Sanctuary"—is one of the most startling moments of all spiritual history, let alone this seven-year period.

Thus it is not the Rapture that calls our attention to this momentous time, but something quite different. It is Satan's attempt to rule the world as God!

In Daniel 7:25 it is clear that the Antichrist and certain believers are meant, and that there will be 3½ years of persecution. But we feel that these 3½ years of persecution refer to the *second* half of the Tribulation. Revelation 13:7 speaks of this same persecution of saints in the atmosphere of the Antichrist's most threatening bid for world control, *after* he has declared himself to be the leader of the world? Certain saints *are* present in the Tribulation, after the church has been Raptured—those 144,000 saints who undertake world evangelism during the Tribulation. By the second half of the Tribulation they surely will have borne some fruit, thereby incurring the vengeful wrath of the Antichrist. It is therefore these saints to whom Daniel is referring in 7:25.

The mid-trib interpretation that the Antichrist's covenant in Daniel 9:27 is made with the church is a serious confusion of the church with Israel, we think. The seventy weeks of Daniel pertain to the Jews—Gabriel tells the Jewish Daniel, "Seventy weeks are determined upon *thy* people and upon *thy* holy city . . ." (Daniel 9:24) at the beginning of this prophetic section. It is the *Jews* who will offer animal sacrifices in their worship (this would be an absurd misconstruction of Christian worship, which commemorates the *end* of animal sacrifices), and it is the *Jews* whose Temple the Antichrist desecrates.

We feel that the mid-trib view must sacrifice a great deal of sound Scriptural interpretation to propagate this unwieldly arrangement of events.

## PARTIAL RAPTURE

This view holds that only part of the church will be taken up at the Rapture before the Tribulation. The rest of the Christians will have to endure the Tribulation on earth.

This thinking emphasizes the importance of holding to a high level of spirituality and anticipation in order to be sanctified enough to qualify for this

highly selective Rapture. Strongly inspirational
Scriptures are referred to:

> But watch thou in all things, endure afflictions, do the
> work of an evangelist, make full proof of thy ministry.
> For I am now ready to be offered, and the time of my
> departure is at hand. I have fought a good fight, I have
> finished my course, I have kept the faith. Henceforth
> there is laid up for me a crown of righteousness, which
> the Lord, the righteous judge, shall give me at that day,
> and not to me only, but unto all them also that love his
> appearing.
>
> —2 Timothy 4:5-8

It is this latter group, those who "love his appearing," who are to be favored with the Rapture and
thereby avoid the Tribulation horrors, according to
the partial-rapture theory. People who are not wait-
ing in proper anticipation for the Lord to come will
be left behind even if they are genuinely born again.

Those who hold this view feel that it provides
great incentive for godly living. But we feel that it
does violence to the whole idea of the Rapture and
the church.

If only a part of the church were to be Raptured,
who would be honored as the Bride of Christ at the
Marriage of the Lamb in heaven (Revelation 19:7-
9)? The completed and perfected church in its en-
tirety is actually to be presented to the Lord on that
great occasion; surely we cannot imagine a "partial
bride"!

The crown which is reserved for those who love
Christ's appearing is not the Rapture but a reward to
be given to *some* believers after *all* of the church has
been Raptured, as determined at the Judgment Seat

of Christ (2 Corinthians 5:10). Paul emphasizes that at the Rapture we shall *all* be changed—all prepared to meet the Lord in resurrection bodies (1 Corinthians 15:51). This seems to apply (since the Apostle made no distinction) to the *entire* church, whether spiritual or carnal, mature or immature. Of course we know that genuine, born-again believers will be separated out of falsely professing "Christians" at the Rapture, but we can find no Biblical segregation in the true church as to strength of belief or effectiveness of ministry, when it comes to the the rapture of God's children.

## PAST-TRIB RAPTURE

This rather unique Rapture theory says that there won't be any future Tribulation period at all because it has already occurred. The Lord is to come in a combined Rapture-second coming, and the Millennium is to get underway immediately. This could virtually happen at once, since there is no seven-year Tribulation to come.

Adherents to this view hold that the seven-year Tribulation period, Daniel's seventieth week, immediately followed the Prophet's first 69 weeks, and that this occurred just after the first advent of Christ.

This view therefore asserts that nothing more is to happen in prophecy before the Lord arrives to accomplish simultaneously the Rapture and start the kingdom. This is similar to the post-trib view in its "unity of the second coming," but it differs in its expectation about the future.

We feel that this theory fails in two serious ways—first, there was no worldwide Tribulation period following the Lord's first advent, and second, the events specified for the genuine Tribulation have not yet happened.

Jesus' description of the "abomination of desolation," the great blasphemy of the Antichrist (Matthew 24: 15) is certainly not to be found in the past. We haven't even seen the Antichrist yet! There was certainly persecution of the believers in the first century (even as now in certain countries), but did this persecution meet Christ's description of "great tribulation . . . such as was not since the beginning of the world to this time, no, nor ever shall be" (Matthew 24:15,21)?

We think this theory fails the test of both history and prophecy.

## NO RAPTURE

The "no-Rapture" people will not highly value this book. They will consider it utterly meaningless from cover to cover.

They feel there will be no Rapture, no Tribulation period, no Armageddon and no Millennium. Their view is very simple—the Lord will return and judge everybody in a general resurrection, and then eternity will begin.

They reason that since the Lord said, "It is not for you to know the times or the seasons, which the Father hath put in his own power" (Acts 1:7), all this prophecy study is a waste of time. The gospel message in its basics is sufficient for them—Christ came and He will return. All who have been saved will fare well.

We need not spend a great deal of time refuting this position, for it ignores vast portions of Scripture in both Old and New Testaments, but it is worth mentioning that events of our present times have already begun to refute this view. We are seeing specific prophecies fulfilled which the "no-Rapture" adherents have always considered meaningless. Before the land of Israel was recovered by the chosen people the "no-Rapture" position was supposed to have been proven, for "how could such a thing ever happen?" But now the Jews have recovered not only the land but also the Temple site (in the 1967 Six-Day War), Russia's animosity has become warlike, and on and on.

Prophecy fulfillment today is a major factor in the present revival of interest in the Bible as a tool for understanding life in general and the complexities of modern life in particular. We have referred to several prophecy books as we have discussed the Rapture in this book, and each of these is a best-seller. Unbelievers buy them as well as Bible students simply because they are so very relevant. It goes without saying that many people have been brought to a saving faith in Christ by the very relevancy of the Biblical messages about our times and the future. It was a major message of the apostles to characterize the fatal differences between people who lived for the world and people who lived for Christ. They based many of their evangelical appeals on what was *going to happen* to each of these groups. They made their points clearly, so that we today can understand them and apply them. It was a great method for building churches back then, and it still is now.

## SUMMARY

We can only repeat that we hold to the pretribulation Rapture as the only reasonable possibility in view of the Scriptural evidence. We have not found a compromise among the positions. We feel that the importance of the Rapture in God's overall plan is of paramount importance to every Christian, and we repeat that we expect it without warning, any day now.

## Chapter 8

# HERE COMES
# THE BRIDE!

*Heaven!!*
*She somehow knew it when she saw it.*

*An instant before, as she had passed through the air in that incredibly euphoric sensation that was the Rapture, she had been stunned and overwhelmed. She had realized at the moment it started happening that she was going up to meet the Lord—she knew this because she had remained ready for it all her life. But then there was a sudden and wonderful moment in which she knew that she was forever changed.*

*Now she looked around her and saw the millions of saints, each one aglow, each one respendent in his new body. All the saints were white and beautiful, and she knew even before she looked that she too now had an incorruptible, eternal body.*

*She knew a lot of things now—she realized, in a peculiar way, that her mind was different too. It was transformed, as the Lord had promised, and she suddenly "knew" her past and her future—she seemed to have a new cognizance of things, and her whole life on earth and her whole future in eternity were "together" in her mind as one scene.*

*She was aware of being surrounded by magnificent joy in the crowd of saints, and in the angels that were gathered around. No one seemed to have to express anything; the joy was just all-pervading, and she was exhilarated by it, practically dizzy with it. This was it!! She was in heaven! She had come to meet her Lord. He had not forgotten her—her place had been prepared.*

*It would have been almost too much for her old mind to bear. As it was, her new mind was full of the wonder and the glory of it all, and she seemed to have a new understanding of the rightness and meaning of it all.*

*The crowd was moving together toward some central point, and she well knew that the Judgment Seat of Christ awaited her presence. She had not known in earthly life whether this was to be anticipated with joy or with dread, but her sensation now was to proceed eagerly to that moment when she would see the Lord face-to-face.*

*When her time came she stepped forward to stand before the King.*

*She was immediately encouraged by His attitude; He seemed to welcome her graciously. Before anything was said her mind was suddenly full of her earthly life; it was flashing by like a high-speed film, but she was conscious of every minute of it. The episodes of her childhood went by, and she recognized dear friends long-forgotten. And then the moment of her coming to the Lord in faith was reviewed, and her heart gladdened until it seemed as if it would burst; God bless that moment, she thought. Without it I wouldn't be standing here in the very presence of my Savior!*

*Her life's events following that moment of conversion were reviewed in great detail, somehow all in an instant, but her new mind was equal to perceiving each event in its fullness. It was an amazing life, presented like this, all in a moment, and she alternated between gladness and aching regret as she beheld her own history.*

*How often she had quenched the Spirit! In 25 years of faith she had failed the Lord again and again, she now saw, until her selfishness, lack of love, and plain meanness seemed to fill her whole mind. But there were good moments too, and she was almost embarrassed before the Lord as her acts of Christian kindness and humility were reviewed. There were small moments when she had done good acts by stealth, and they were all in the picture. There were times when she had carried out the Lord's commands when it had been very hard to do. There were times when she could have sinned greatly, but she had chosen the Lord's way instead. There were times when her faith had shown through—when she cared for the poor and the lost sheep—and times of intercession, when she had poured out her heart to God on behalf of the church, of the missionaries, and of all the Lord's works on earth.*

*She realized, in her new way of knowing things, that her good works were to be enshrined for all eternity and that her bad works were to be burned* up like old soiled rags. For this she was grateful; her life, she realized would not have stood up to the test of the King before her had He not arranged beforehand to nullify her sins.

A multifaceted crown was placed upon her head then, and she emerged from the throne of grace regally, with a new perspective of herself and the endless road of joy ahead of her. The judgment was over and heaven was hers!

Then there was a scene of great solemnity and triumph as the gathered believers admired each other's crowns and exulted in their collective joy. Everyone was overwhelmed by a fact that stood out very obviously for each of them; all of this had become possible—their very crowns, their magnificent deliverance—only through the sacrifice of their King.

It was His singular life that passed through their minds now; He had come to bring salvation to all men, and love, and joy, and peace. But He had been whipped and stabbed and crucified. His resurrection was now shared with them, so that their lesser actions had been burned up for all time as they stood crowned like kings themselves.

She felt a desire to pay further homage to the Lord then, and she stepped forward, as did the others, to lay her crown at His feet. The throng came to the throne, in devotion and gratitude, lifting their crowns and presenting them at the foot of the throne. The gathered saints began a heartfelt song, "Worthy is the Lamb that was slain. . . ."

After that initial ceremony, which she knew was only a small picture of the endless joy and kindness that would forever reign in her life now, she began to get acquainted with her many new neighbors and friends. It was a joyous community indeed, and she now knew where her old mind had gotten its ideas of what life could be like if only we really did love one another.

She received a wedding invitation!

She knew it all along; she was to be part of the Bride of Christ, and there was indeed a joyous wedding in the making. She had prepared with excitement for many weddings in her time, but none had ever been like this one! For one thing, the guest list ran into the millions. And for another, she was at last to become the bride of perfect love.

She was so excited she thought she would shout with joy when at last the whole "bride," the church, was assembled. There stood the Bridegroom, at the altar before His Father, and the entire church massed to be united with the Lord. The believers of the Old Testament age were also gathered, and she somehow was able to recognize honored wedding guests Abraham and David and the others. Would this incredible joy ever cease?

She knew the answer to that!

The angels glowed with pleasure as the Lord at last took His bride in heavenly marriage and the church was fulfilled.

She had been only dimly conscious, through all of this, of the sad events happening on the earth below. She well knew, without being consciously aware of it, that there was more to be done down there, since her new Husband was to continue perfecting His creation.

There remained only the event of her trip back to the earth with the Lord and the rest of His Bride to set up the kingdom, of which she used to pray, "Thy will be done on earth, as it is in heaven."

Really, we know very little about heaven.

But we Christians "walk by faith, not by sight," as Paul put it (2 Corinthians 5:7). Intimations in the Scriptures about heaven give us at least a great appreciation of that wonderful place, if not exact details. The Christian longs to go to heaven to be with the Lord, to be with loved ones who have gone on before, to be finished with this life of sin, toil, and sorrow, and to rest at last in glory.

When a Christian dies, his death is different from that of unbelievers. His body is buried, but his soul goes to the presence of the Lord (2 Corinthians 5:6-9). At the time of the Rapture, that soul will be reunited with its former body and resurrected. The transformation to immortality will take place then, and the believer will live on eternally.

Those alive at the moment of the Rapture will be translated directly and changed at once, without ever experiencing death.

Thus at the time of the Rapture, both the resurrected and the translated saints will be carried away from the earth in eternal bodies to join Christ in heaven.

It's not very easy for us earth-lubbers to describe these marvels, of course, other than to take the facts from the Word and write them out. But faith in the revealed facts makes a big difference in the earthly life of any believer. Paul's point is well taken that we do not have to actually see a Christian thing to believe in it; Christians experience so many spiritual, "mystical" transactions in their daily walk that heaven is not at all hard to believe in.

In walking by faith we gain a serenity and assurance that is simple unexplainable to the rest of the world. That we count on a blessed "hereafter" has confounded many kinds of thinkers ever since the gospel times themselves. The Christian confidence about death has caused many people to wonder.

The Marxists have called Christianity "the opiate of the masses," since masses who count on a bright future seem drugged to them! To them heaven has become a delusion, an escapist way of thinking, and an impractical utopia. Believers have been regarded as folks who turn their attention from the hard realities of the here-and-now to concentrate on some theoretical better life to come. Psychologists theorize that a future heaven makes life on earth more endurable, and so the naive Christians like to persuade themselves that their belief is true.

Actually, of course, the experience of true faith in

God provides reliable and intimate assurances of heaven every day. True Christians are familiar with real joy, and they taste heaven-like blessings by faith every day. The abundant life given by Christ far exceeds the physical life understood by the five senses, and it speaks clearly and reasonably of a continuing blessing after death.

To the Christian, the realities of heaven are more dependable than those of the earthly life. The things which we see here on earth are temporary, we know, but the things which are now invisible will last forever. (2 Corinthians 4:18). It's a backwards kind of philosophy to the materialistic, earthbound thinker, but it has only to be tried to be verified.

Thus Christians wait in faith to be delivered—to be taken away to heaven. There, we know from Scripture, is the kind of life believers were meant to live! There in heaven is joy, peace, love, and glory in the very presence of God Himself.

The first event of our existence in heaven, however, is one which causes mixed emotions among believers for all Christians will be judged at the judgment seat of Christ (2 Corinthians 5:10). This will be the scene of an examination of each Christian life by the Lord Himself. On that day Christians will see what they have done and not done, and how it all looks from heaven's perspective.

This heavenly judgment should certainly not be confused with what is popularly called "Judgment Day," that final judgment of all unbelievers who have ever lived. That ultimate judgment will be held at the conclusion of the Millennium, and it will involve penalties and loss of life. Jesus' judgment seat, on the other hand, examines only the *works* of believers, not the believers themselves:

For we must all appear before the judgment seat of Christ, that everyone may receive the things done in his body, according to what he hath done, whether good or bad.

—2 Corinthians 5:10

Every man's work shall be made manifest, for the day shall declare it, because it shall be revealed by fire; and the fire shall try every man's work, of what sort it is. If any man's work abide which he hath built thereupon, he shall receive a reward.
If any man's work shall be burned, he shall suffer loss: *but he himself shall be saved,* yet so as by fire.

—1 Corinthians 3:13-15

The issue at this judgment seat is not condemnation or even punishment. No one need fear the Lord's wrath or need worry about his salvation at this event. For believers, those issues were taken care of on the cross by the Judge Himself. First Corinthians 3:15 stresses that a believer and his works are two different things in the sight of the Lord.

This judgment has to do more with rewards than with punishments. We will be "receiving the things done in our body" in other words, we will be receiving the results of our earthly lives. This refers to the way we have served our Lord on earth during the time that we knew Him.

Our works of service for the Lord vary a great deal, of course, and we're going to know just how much they vary on that unique day in heaven when the Lord looks all of them over. Some works will be extremely pleasing to Him and others not at all. And even within these two groups of good works and bad works there will be gradations: good works will be graded as "gold, silver, and precious stones," while bad works will be graded as "wood, hay, and stubble" (1 Corinthians 3:12).

Paul's image of the testing of our works (". . . it shall be revealed by fire and the fire shall try every man's work, of what sort it is") is very logical. The precious metals and jewels will survive the fire while the wood, hay, and stubble will be totally consumed. It is as if the entire works of our lifetimes in Christ will be piled up and put to the torch. What comes out of that fire will last for eternity; what is burned will be gone forever.

On earth we burn our trash to get rid of it. How good it will be to permanently get rid of *all* our earthly trash!

The things that last—the good works—are pictured as beautiful rather than merely durable; they are *precious and beautiful* things rather than durable but drab iron and stone. In Paul's metaphor is the intimation that we will be adorned with our good works for all eternity. We are to "wear" them in glory!

The Lord made each one of us, and He knows how we tick. Our salvation does not depend on these good works; it is a free gift. But the opportunity is open for us to earn rewards for good service. By God's grace we can work to receive that finest of commendations from the very lips of the Lord Himself, "Well done, thou good and faithful servant."

We are not expected, of course, to be able to perform works pleasing to Almighty God by our own strength. It is by the grace of God that we produce these durable works—by our yielding to His direction, just as a good servant yields to his master's will. As we yield to God, He produces good works in us that we send on to heaven, as it were, and these become our "treasures in heaven." Jesus recommended that our personal fortunes be stored above, where they are safe, rather than on the earth, where thieves break in and steal.

God is practical; He even operates a sound retirement program! We contribute now and reap the benefits later on. Our pension fund is safe and sound under God's own care in heaven!

No one can be sure how long the Judgment Seat will last, or even on how we reckon time in heaven, but in earthly terms all heavenly business must be cleared up in seven years. That is, the Tribulation will be wracking the earth for a seven-year period, and the heavenly events scheduled to occur before Christ's second coming must be accomplished during this seven-year period. What a difference between heaven and earth! There will be joy above but woe below, and such extremes between the two!

The wedding of Christ and His bride, the church, plus the Marriage Supper of the Lamb, will take place after the Judgment Seat events. An actual wedding ceremony will be held in heaven, and it will surely be something to behold!

The bride will wish to present the bridegroom with a "dowry," and so the members of the church will give to Christ their only possessions—their crowns. While the crowns are made to last for eternity, it appears that the church does not keep them, but rather presents them to the Bridegroom with the proclamation that He alone is worthy of praise (Revelation 4:10, 11; 5:11, 12).

"Let us be glad and rejoice, and give honor to him, for the marriage of the Lamb is come, and his wife hath made herself ready. And to her was granted that she should be arrayed in fine linen, clean and white; for the fine linen is the righteousness of saints." This is how Revelation 19:7,8 sings about this unique, joyful moment of heavenly matrimony.

It is admittedly difficult to imagine this idea of a corporate wedding of the church to the Lord. The church is composed of millions of individuals, but apparently in heaven it becomes one personality clothed in beauty, chastity, purity, and loveliness, with her entire yearning and aspiration to be presented in this fashion to her Bridegroom, the Lord Jesus Christ. An actual ceremony is envisioned, with the Father conducting the marriage, the Son standing as a literal Bridegroom, the Holy Spirit escorting the redeemed church as the Bride, and the wedding guests being the innumerable spirits of the Old Testament saints.

This is the ceremony toward which Christ has been looking for almost 2000 years now, and really from eternity past. It was at least partly for this unique, mystic event that He endured the Cross. He surely anticipates this wedding at least as much as does his stumbling, erring, unchaste church today.

The wedding ceremony, though not given a great deal of space in Scripture, is certainly one of the preeminent events of God's program for His own. We don't completely understand what a heavenly wedding is, especially between the Savior and the millions, but we all know what marriage is. It is as if the Lord wishes to create a relationship with his own people which is more intimate, more complete, more loving, and more adoring than any He has participated in previously. Marriage, the ultimate union, the final joining together, will be accomplished in heaven as it never was on earth—God's relations with men, even with Israel, were never so close as this.

In Revelation 19:9 a "Marriage Supper" is spoken of, and this is generally thought to be just that—a kind of reception meal following the wedding. It has also been suggested that this supper will be delayed until after Christ descends to the earth and establishes His Kingdom. In the latter case the Marriage Supper would correspond with the millennial banquet described by Isaiah (25:6-8).

Whether or not the two suppers are the same or are held successively, the church and the rest of the redeemed of all ages are in for some joyful feasting. The Lord enjoyed a good meal, as we do, and He has made many many plans along these lines.

So the Bride of Christ will be completed in heaven, attired graciously and presented to her Bridegroom. She will be formally wed and will return triumphantly to the earth with her Lord and Husband to establish and reign over the millennial kingdom of God.

## Chapter 9

# COMIN' FOR TO CARRY ME HOME

*He was very tired, but very joyful.*

*He had made the big step.*

*He now belonged to Jesus Christ. He was now a Christian.*

*He sat at his desk, the surface covered with books about prophecy, and reflected on his decision. It had been the only reasonable course. Sure, he would face some derision now from his unbelieving friends. He would be called a "Holy Roller" and a "Jesus Freak," but he had studied the matter fairly and he had reached the only rational conclusion. Jesus was alive and He was coming back.*

*It had started a few weeks before, when one of his good friends began "witnessing" to him. At first he had asked his friend to lay off, to let these spiritual matters alone. Life was full of mysteries, and he had been content at that time just to let this particular one go on being mysterious. There were times in the past when he'd frankly envied his friend, whose faith seemed so sustaining and who got so much out of his religious life. He'd watched as his friend prospered at his work, at his church, and in his family life. But he'd always attributed that to just "clean living" or whatever—anything but faith in Christ.*

*For his own part, he'd always felt more comfortable looking at life as simply inexplicable and therefore interesting in its own right. The Bible was too vague, and his friend's explanations were too pat. Things were surely not as simple as that. It wasn't that he felt God had died—he just wondered if God had ever lived.*

*But his friend had patiently gotten him interested in a new area of Bible study—prophecy. He'd had to admit it—the Bible seemed very knowledgeable about current events. It was uncanny, but he began to get the feeling that the prophets were right, and that there was a whole other dimension to life that he had neglected. Morality was still, in his mind, largely a matter of opinion, but only a fool would ignore cogent analyses of his own future.*

*So he'd gone with his faithful friend to a Christian bookstore and had brought home a stack of current books on prophecy and the world situation.*

*And now his desk was awash in Christian books and he looked like some sort of theologian. Where he had previously read only a few current novels and some popular paperbacks, he had now turned into a student of Christian literature. The works of Lindsey, Pentecost, Feinberg, Walvoord, and other prophecy writers of the day were his new bill of fare.*

*McCall and Levitt, who wrote like newspaper reporters out of the future, had fascinated him no end!*

*Titles like* Things to Come, The Late Great Planet Earth, Armageddon, *and* Satan in the Sanctuary *had replaced his pop fiction, and for once he was becoming very knowledgeable about where he and the rest of the world were going.*

*He had learned more than prophecy. All of these books had emphasized the utter necessity of a personal relationship with Jesus Christ. The knowledge would not have profited him very much without that, because in any case he would fall prey to the Antichrist if he were not lined up with the Lord. Somehow the way they put it made sense, and one quiet night he had come to the realization that Jesus had indeed died for his sins. He realized that God loved him with a kind of love that sacrificed everything. He understood that he had a responsibility to receive this great love. Overwhelmed and grateful, he had made his peace with God and received Jesus as his Lord and Savior.*

*And now he felt a great peace. He would not be a dominated subject of the Antichrist's world government scheme. He would not fall prey to Satan. He knew, as well as he had ever known anything, that the Lord would come for him before any of that came to pass. He was truly a new creature in Christ, and his sense of struggle with life was over.*

*Now his new fascination was the topic of the Rapture. He had seen the Biblical references to it and he had read the explanations of it in the various books on prophecy he was studying. He understood that the Lord would come suddenly and that His coming was imminent.*

*He reached for his cup of coffee beside his books*

---

*on the desk, but his hand barely touched the cup. His glasses fell to the desk, his clothing dropped limp on the chair. He heard a shout . . . a trumpet!*

*Suddenly, all in a moment, "in the twinkling of an eye," he was . . . gone!*

---

Are you a Gentile, a Jew, or a Christian?

According to the Bible, you belong to one of these three groups, and your future depends on which one.

This book, for the most part, has been a tale of these three peoples and their different destinies, and we have said all we could in the space available. God has revealed remarkable things about His coming dealings with these three distinctly different segments of the world's population, and we have tried to clarify these dealings as we understand them. We depend entirely, of course, on the Bible for our various conclusions.

The Gentiles, as we have said, cannot reasonably look to a bright future. In prophecy it is clear that the unbelieving Gentiles will follow the coming Antichrist, the world ruler of the Tribulation. He will take them down the primrose path to destruction. His political, economic, and religious plans will lead only to Armageddon.

Further on down the prophetic road the Gentiles will face judgment and will fare no better than Satan himself, according to the Bible. The Lake of Fire awaits all unbelievers—fallen angels and unregenerate men alike.

If you are a Gentile, bound and determined to remain in disbelief, your only hope is that the Biblical picture of things is false. But if only *half* of what the Bible predicts really does happen, some very hard times lie ahead for you. (Of course we feel that every detail of the Bible is wholly accurate; in giving you the benefit of the doubt, we still find matters hopeless!)

The Jews will fare somewhat better, at least as a nation, if not as individuals. They are seen prophetically as a very special people, divinely chosen but presently separated from both their land and their Lord. They are just as lost, in this separated condition, as the Gentiles, but ultimately their double exile will end.

As we have seen, the Jews will yet return en masse to the land and to the Lord. God has promised that at the sound of the trumpet He will regather His chosen people from the ends of the earth and return them to Israel. That won't be a happy time, of course, since the Tribulation will be underway. But this "time of Jacob's trouble" is limited and has a divine purpose. The nation of Israel will be purified as if by fire, and the Jewish people will be ready when the Messiah returns.

From then on, Israel and Jerusalem will receive

the greatest of honors as their glorious destiny is fulfilled. The Lord will reign a thousand years in Jerusalem, and the Promised Land will become the head of a grand world of peaceful nations.

But being a Jew at this moment does not guarantee safe passage to the Millennium. The unsaved Jew, like the unsaved Gentile, must confront the Antichrist and his heinous seven-year rule. Many Jews will die, and they'll be dead men forever.

Christians, on the other hand, have little to fear from the future. Let's understand again what a Christian is—a Jew or Gentile who believes in Jesus Christ.

Christians constitute another chosen people of God, selected for a definite bright future. The Christians, or the church, are for the moment in exile like the Jews, but the trumpet will signal their complete and ultimate triumph. The church will go home to heaven in the Rapture, be joined to the Lord in marriage, and return with Him to reign.

After the millennial kingdom the church will continue with the Lord into the mystical period of eternity, in which there will be instituted a new heaven, a new earth, and a New Jerusalem. The church will live on in glory and triumph with the Lord.

These scenarios are, in brief, what the Scriptures have to say about the three groups of people now present in the world.

To which group do you belong? More to the point, should you consider making a change?

There's actually only one group you can change to. Biblically, a Gentile cannot become a Jew and a Jew cannot become a Gentile. But anybody, just anybody, can become a Christian. In fact, God is utterly anxious about it; He wants everybody to be in the church. "I have no pleasure in the death of him that dieth," says the Father in Ezekiel 18:32. "Wherefore turn yourselves, and live ye." He says, "Seek and ye shall find," "Knock and it shall be opened unto you," "Ask and it shall be given."

God's attitude is very clear.

But God's attitude counts less on this matter than your own attitude. He didn't make you as a puppet that He could control, but He gave you a free choice. You are free to go with Him or to go the other way. Your future really depends on you.

Our personal view of the Rapture is really less technical than we have presented it here. We have tried to give every detail of the event, even the views we don't personally hold, in order to expose the entire subject to consideration. But most of the time we think about this whole beautiful event in much more simple terms.

When we think about the Rapture we think about the sweet lyric that says, "Comin' for to carry me home."

You see, once you're on the other side of this faith question—once you're lined up with the Lord—it all becomes very simple and very comfortable. He's coming for us, and that's all there is to it. What will happen to the world is too bad, but our Lord is coming to carry us home and we're glad. He has paid our way, arranged the trip, and reserved our places.

He can do as much for you.

Think about it. It will be the most important decision you'll ever make.

The Lord knows you very well. He made you, just

as you are. You can talk to him in your own words. And He'll certainly listen.

If heaven is the home you want, and if you want to go there in the Rapture, it's very easy. Just believe God's Word. Believe that His Son, the Messiah Jesus, died for your sins, as He said He did, and that He now lives to provide eternal life for you. There's no charge.

If your own words fail you, here's some of ours that we can recommend:

> Lord, I want to be ready for the Rapture. Come for me and carry me home! Let me be a part of Your Bride in heaven. I believe that Your death and resurrection were for me, and I want You to be the head of my life from now on. I appreciate all You have done for me, and You will do for me in the future. Thanks.

The first thing you saw when you picked up this book was the picture on the cover. There was nobody in that picture. You know now, having read this book, why there was nobody in that picture. He just left. He's gone. He was Raptured.

Our prayer is that you too may be missing from that picture some great day!